THE LEADERSHIP ADVENTURE

Five powerful secrets every leader should
Know to motivate people & maximise productivity

HITEN BHATT

Reviews of The Leadership Adventure

"If you are serious about growing as a Leader, then you really should read this book. Hiten's Leadership Adventure is an exciting and transformative one. He coaches you in a very engaging way throughout this book to really think about leadership in a unique way and make a difference to your business!"

Olu Orugboh – Managing Director, Synergy Organisational Solutions

"The Leadership Adventure is a very powerful and practical book that every leader should read. The five secrets are simple truths that we all know that we should be doing as leaders, but we can often forget in the day to day running of a business. Hiten's book makes you think and take stock of what is really important."

Alan Barratt, MBA, DMS, BA (Hons), FCMI – Head of Supply Chain, Cox Automotive UK

"Hiten is a powerful coach that can really get your team aligned and help you focus as a leader on what is important. His coaching has really helped my team at MSDUK to clarify their personal and professional goals. We are now growing our next generation of leaders and taking the business to our next stage of growth, with a fully motivated and driven team."

Mayank Shah – CEO MSDUK

"Leadership has been analysed, studied and dissected by experts for years with lots of ideas about what makes an effective leader. I feel that Hiten's book, The Leadership Adventure offers leaders a unique introspective insight that turns the focus on the leader themselves, if more leaders followed the principles in this book the world would be a happier place."

Michel Laurent-Regisse – Leader Advisor, Leicester City Council

"Hiten is a gifted coach with the ability to connect to people. I have personally witnessed the massive positive life transformations that have occurred as a result of Hiten's training workshops. The Leadership Adventure is a book that can powerfully move you from negativity and doubt into motivation, positivity and action, I recommend it for every leader."
Mat Jesson – Leader and Team Coordinator, The Prince's Trust

"Hiten's Leadership Adventure will aid you to become a more effective, emotionally intelligent and strategic leader by helping you understand your own behaviour as a fundamental starting point."
Ghanshyam Ramparia – Entrepreneur and Investor

"The leadership adventure is a thought provoking book that is written to help you think more about leadership and your role in it. This book is about the human side of business and leadership, I encourage you to read it."
Lesley Tull - Vice President Human Resources, Danfoss

About the Author

Hiten Bhatt is a powerful, motivational speaker, leadership and life coach. Hiten's training seminars and coaching workshops are unique, transformational experiences that have positively impacted businesses and changed the lives of individuals. Hiten, previously worked in the legal profession and left his career in law to pursue his calling, teaching leaders from all walks of life and backgrounds, from CEOs, senior executives, entrepreneurs, professional athletes, teachers, parents and young people how they can give their true gift to the world and unleash their true potential. He delivers his brand of magic with humour, play and deep practical insight. He is the founder of BE GREAT Training, a business built on the principle that learning, growth and improvement is an exciting adventure of discovery that never ends. Hiten often asks leaders an interesting question, if living things grow, and you are not growing, what are you?

Foreword

I believe business is about people and relationships, and Hiten's book brings this powerful, fundamental idea to life. The heart of leadership is the leadership of the heart and this book will transform the way you approach being a leader, whether it is in your professional or personal life. Entrepreneurship for me is a very exciting journey and it has certainly been challenging at times, leading my business forwards over the years is an adventure and that is exactly what leadership is, an adventure, where you learn more about yourself in the process and grow as an individual. Hiten is a gifted coach and throughout this book he teaches you the principles of successful leadership in a way that is engaging, fun and effective.

As leaders, we all want to motivate people and maximise the productivity of our teams to get the most out of our people. I believe this is part art and part science with a heavy dose of application and Hiten lays out some of the solid foundations in this book. Any leader should embark upon building stronger relationships with their peer groups around them. This book is powerful and practical, it will make you think and be a useful tool to make you a better leader.

Byron Dixon
Award Winning Entrepreneur
CEO, Micro-Fresh International

A Chemist by profession, Byron Dixon, is the founder and owner of the Leicester based, award winning, antimicrobial business, Corium Solutions Ltd. Corium Solutions develops a formula to stop goods from getting mouldy. Byron has developed an innovative anti-fungal treatment called Micro-Fresh®. Some of the largest UK retailers such as NEXT, John Lewis and Kickers are all using Micro-Fresh® brand and technology to promote enhanced 'freshness' as a marketing edge in footwear, bedding and clothing. He is a graduate of the coveted Goldman Sachs 10,000 Small Businesses UK Programme and was selected to join the Aspiring Entrepreneurs Programme at the Peter Jones Academy, amongst many other achievements. Byron is also a fellow of Aston University and an active collaborator in community projects working with disadvantaged young people.

Dedication

This book is dedicated to both of my Gurus, His Holiness Pramukh Swami Maharaj and His Holiness Mahant Swami Maharaj. *'In the joy of others lies our own'*, was the profound statement that Pramukh Swami Maharaj not only spoke but lived, he was a true leader in every sense of the word. Today his spiritual successor, Mahant Swami Maharaj and the present head of BAPS Swaminarayan Sanstha, travels the world teaching the principles of harmony, empathy and unity, which are so important for leaders to imbibe in today's world. Mahant Swami often says that one should strive to be a servant of a servant, this is leadership at its most sublime height, to serve others without ego or expectations. I humbly dedicate this book at their divine feet and pray that I can earn their innermost blessings.

Acknowledgements

First and foremost, I acknowledge both my Gurus, His Holiness Pramukh Swami Maharaj and His Holiness Mahant Swami Maharaj with whose blessings everything is possible. I would like to thank my parents and family, my very supportive wife Poonam and daughter, Varni-Bhakti, a great leader already! A special thanks to Sagar Rathod and Tilak Parmar, two young leaders and dynamic entrepreneurs who are destined to do great things. I would also like to thank my book coach and mentor, Vishal Morjaria whose fantastic Wow Book Camp has helped me to complete this book in a faster time than I thought possible.

I thank Lyndsay Hill of The Brown Fox Bureau for her great editing skills. Thank you to Nikesh Gudka for his helpful suggestions, Priya Tailor for her amazing creativity and design skills as well as Kalpesh Chauhan for his support with printing. A heartfelt thanks to Byron Dixon for writing the foreword and Jigna Varu and the team at Micro – Fresh for their support. Thank you to all the great entrepreneurs and business leaders that have contributed a testimonial in this book. Thank you to my friends and family and to everyone who has been part of my journey so far!

Note to the Reader

The information, including opinion and analysis, contained herein are based on the author's personal experiences and is not intended to provide professional advice. The author and the publisher make no warranties, either expressed or implied, concerning the accuracy, applicability, effectiveness, reliability or suitability of the contents. If you wish to apply or follow the advice or recommendations mentioned herein, you take full responsibility for your actions. The author and publisher of this book shall in no circumstances be held liable for any direct, indirect, incidental or consequential damages arising directly or indirectly from the use of any of the information contained in this book. All content is for information only and is not warranted for content accuracy or any other implied or explicit purpose.

TAKE YOUR LEADERSHIP SKILLS TO THE NEXT LEVEL

The Leadership Adventures™ is a powerful engaging programme, that will transform you as an individual, your team and your organization.

To find out how you, your business, or your organization can benefit from the Leadership Adventures Training Program
Email: info@BeGreatTraining.com

CONTENTS

Chapter 1

THE POWER OF WHY

This book contains five powerful secrets that can be used to motivate people and ensure you bring out the best in them. It is a book for anyone who finds themselves in a leadership position and wants to do a better job. We are all leaders! If you are a parent you are a leader to your child. If you have a spouse, partner or friend you will at times be their leader and, of course, in your career or business if you are responsible for a team, you are again a leader. Leadership extends into all areas of life and developing great leadership qualities in people is vital for organizations and the business world to stay ahead of the competition and really maximize productivity, profits and results. Developing your own great leadership qualities will be a deeply rewarding and transformative experience, with amazing benefits that extend far beyond what you actually achieve within in your career or business.

What is the definition of a secret? Something that is not known or seen, or not meant to be known or seen by anyone else. If you know something but do not actually apply it, that is as good as being a secret. The ideas in this book are based on one fundamental truth, that in leading a family, leading people in a small to medium sized business, or leading multinational teams in a global corporate organization, is essentially about understanding human beings; understanding human behaviour and understanding human relationships. If you do not understand this, you do not understand business or life at its deepest levels! The ideas contained in this book are very simple but are very powerful and effective. The self-reflection questions at the end of each chapter are there for you to really take the time to think and reflect on your learnings, so that you can apply what you have learnt in your interactions with others and really begin the journey of becoming a great leader. Let us begin by examining the first powerful secret of leadership, the power of **WHY**.

The human animal instinct is truly fascinating! What is it that separates man from all the other species in the world? An advanced ability to think, create and apply meaning to life? Throughout human history this ability has been used for good and evil. This ability to apply meaning to life is what makes us fundamentally human, even in the most horrific of situations. In his book, *Man's Search for Meaning* by Victor Frankl, a survivor of the horrors of the Nazi concentration camps during World War II, he makes a powerful statement. . .

"Everything can be taken from a man but one thing: the last of the human freedoms—to choose one's attitude in any given set of circumstances, to choose one's own way."

Human beings have an amazing ability to apply meaning to the events that happen to them in life. In the case of Victor Frankl, even something as dehumanizing as the concentration camps did not stop him from finding a temporary escape and respite in his mind, in his imagination and memories. Human beings need meaning, need purpose, they need a strong WHY behind their life and activities. The WHY generates passion, it is the *'fire in the belly'*, it is the key to encouraging excitement, motivation and for the leader to bring out the best in their people, for their own good and the good of the business or organization.

Understanding Their WHY

Have you seen people day to day acting as we term *'the living dead'*? Have you seen people commuting to work with a miserable expression written all over their faces? They walk into the office or the factory floor at 9.00am, lifeless, but prepared to embark on another meaningless day at work. It's the same story at school when you observe the *'bored out of their brains'* students sitting in class just waiting for the end of school. How productive, in terms of quality output, do you think these employees or students will be? How loyal and committed do you believe they are to their workplaces, organizations or schools?

The job of the great leader is to raise the dead! The great leader is the one who can harness the power of WHY by understanding their team, employees, family members or students by understanding: What gets them excited? What are they passionate about? What is important to them? The lifeless employee suddenly comes back to life at 5.00pm, when they leave the office, happier to go and spend time on social activities, hobbies and interests which they are extremely happy to carry out and are dedicated to. The bored student in school comes to life at home time, fully animated and enthusiastic, laughing and joking with their friends and ready to engage fully in their own interests. There is a clear disconnect between who they are in their personal lives and who they are at work or school. You may argue of course there is a disconnect as, after all, work is work and play is play.

However, imagine, if the people you lead in your family life, business, or team could bring some of the same passion, enthusiasm, diligence and energy they have for their own hobbies and interests, to their work? It would transform your business or organization. WHY do these people show so much passion when it comes to their personal lives and interests? The answer to this is not rocket science!

The answer usually incorporates one, or more, of the following reasons:

- They have a sense of meaning, purpose and/or challenge from the activity they enjoy;
- It's fun and/or pleasurable to do and creates a feeling of happiness;

- They are supporting, or contributing, to others or a wider cause in some way, giving them a sense of accomplishment and satisfaction.

Great leaders who use the power of why to really get the best out of others, do two very important things. Firstly, they actively find out what '*floats the boat*' of the people they lead, that is to say they find out people's passions and interests. Secondly, they find a way of connecting this natural sense of motivation to their roles in the workplace, organization or team. Meaning, purpose, challenge, fun, pleasure, happiness and contribution are the powerful drivers of motivation and productivity of human beings across cultures. Great leaders find out other people's WHY and then harness and channel that energy towards the goals of the organization or business.

Questioning and Coaching

The bottom line and what really matters, is results. We live in an increasingly complex, fast paced, competitive world with businesses and organizations focusing on profits, outputs and hard measurable data and so they should! However, it is just as important in HOW a business achieves its results and outputs, the journey is just as vital as the destination. The traditional stereotype of a supervisor or manager has been one of hierarchy, a bullish type man, high up in command, in his plush office, instilling fear into his subordinates with no interest or respect for their personal lives. This type of leader is unapproachable and his only focus is on results, he views his people as robots or machines. It is an unfortunate reality that these types of leaders exist everywhere, throughout businesses and organizations of all types, in our schools and universities and sadly within many families; the truth is they end up doing more harm than good.

The leader that subscribes to the Machiavellian philosophy in that 'the ends justify the means', often does achieve results in the short term, however, in the long term they end up costing the organization far more. Many research studies have shown time and again that one of the primary reasons for people leaving their jobs is due to inappropriate behaviour from a supervisor or manager or general poor management. Disengaged employees also often suffer from stress related illnesses and are often absent from work due to long term sickness. How much do you think employee absenteeism, or the need to regularly recruit new staff to replace the old ones, can cost an organization or business? In the long term all of this ends up being very costly indeed!

Perhaps a leader has all the best intentions in the world but just does not have the time to build deeper relationships with their team members, staff or colleagues, after all finding out each individual's WHY takes time, a luxury many are unable to achieve in the working day. However, this type of leader can be just as damaging as the 'bad boss'. Imagine a father that is working every given hour to provide for his family, his intention being to want to ensure his wife and children have the best of everything in life; a nice home, great luxuries and comforts, exciting holidays and the ability to put their children through the best schools and universities, giving them the best chance in life. The father's intentions are meaningful and good but in the process of working so hard, he never takes his child to the park, is never home for bed time, has no time to take his wife for dinner and generally spends little quality time with his family. There is the risk that one day he will return from work, tired and exhausted to find an empty house and a note on the kitchen table, telling him that his wife has decided to leave him and seek a divorce! The children are now teenagers and they care little about their dad because they do not really know him and more importantly, he does not know the first thing about them!

The powerful lesson to be learnt from the above story applies just as much to the business world as it does to one's family life. The lesson is simple, but the importance of it cannot be stressed enough. Great leaders make an investment of their own time and effort to build deeper relationships with their people by getting to know them and understand them. The leader simply has to ask the right questions and listen.

Three effective coaching questions a leader might ask are:
- What do you do outside of work and why is that important to you?
- What are your goals, dreams and ambitions in your work and your life?

- What would bring you more satisfaction in carrying out your current work role and associated duties?

Asking the right questions through a coaching approach can really uncover people's WHY and their deeper motivations. Sometimes you will have to dig a little deeper to uncover their real WHY, for example, if the question *'what would bring more satisfaction to your current role?'* is answered with a need for high remuneration, the next question should be why more money is important to them. You then continue this line of questioning until you hit upon the real deeper reason for wanting more money. The beauty of this approach is that the leader does not necessarily have to suddenly provide a pay rise! However, asking these types of questions and listening carefully to the answers, makes people feel like the leader cares, they listen and understand. The reason, in truth, may be that they would like a fancy car or an exotic holiday, something they need to work for, but what if it is a sick child who requires medical treatment. The answers will allow a more effective line of communication between employer and employee, after all home life effects work life. When people feel understood, they feel that they can trust their leaders and this simple truth does wonders for teams, businesses and families.

Connecting their WHY with your WHY

Great leaders are experienced in asking the right questions and listening to the answers. Many organizations and businesses recognise the importance of providing fantastic customer or client service. They understand very clearly that this focus on the customer or client, builds their brand and reputation and ultimately translates into profitability for the business by attracting more customers and clients. People expect good customer service in this modern era, they like to feel important and be treated fairly. It is an unfortunate shame that many organizations and businesses appear unable to recognize the importance of their 'internal customers', those people who are the team, the workforce, the cogs that make the whole wheel turn. Look after your people and they will look after you, a very simple but often forgotten principle of leadership.

Connecting their WHY with your WHY comes down to the leader's ability to communicate and to follow through with actions. What the business needs is not to be at odds with their employees but rather for the leader to be able to connect the dots and communicate a powerful and compelling vision that really reaches the shared aspirations of the organization and its people. A great leader starts by fundamentally understanding that people need meaning and purpose in their careers and day to day jobs. The result will be the ability to powerfully connect the individual's deeper WHY with the organization's WHY for existing, in others words WHY do we do what we do? The answer '*to make more money*' is simply not powerful or compelling enough to really inspire people to bring their best mood to work, or commit with absolute loyalty to the vision and mission of the organization.

The problem is that businesses and organizations are very good at explaining WHAT they do, they are also very good at explaining HOW they operate, but they are also often unable to, or very poorly, articulate WHY they are doing it. For example, a car manufacturer may communicate how the car operates and explain all its features, they may also detail how the car is made and all the processes involved; they can tell you how many cars they have sold, how many they need to sell and all the facts and figures around the business; however, to really inspire and get the most out of the employees, the communication needs to be deeper, it needs to tell them why they are making this car in the first place.

'We aim to make the safest, most affordable family car so every day working families feel safe, comfortable and happy on the road.'

-or-

'Our luxury sports car seeks to implement the best in technology and aesthetics because we want to create cars that are a beautiful blend of science and art so that we can push our own limits of what is possible and constantly grow.'

In both of these statements the leader is connecting to a deeper purpose, a deeper WHY, the human need for security and the human need for growth and pushing boundaries. In your own leadership role, begin to think about the deeper human WHY for your businesses or organization's existence and begin with communicating this WHY constantly; the WHAT and the HOW are important but not as powerful in moving people than being able to connect to the WHY.

Not Forgetting WHY

As well as working with very successful entrepreneurs, business owners and corporate organizations throughout the world, my work also involves helping disadvantaged young people develop a more successful orientated mindset together with leadership skills in order to better their lives and elevate themselves out of a life of poverty and crime. Ever since they were born, many of these teenagers have never experienced anything other than negativity and hate, with many joining gangs as this 'gang culture' provides a sense of belonging and identity, the gang becomes the closest thing to a family some of them have ever known.

I was delivering a set of workshops with a group of such young people in the UK recently and there was one young man in particular who stood out from the rest of the group. He was a tall, physically strong, tough looking young man and exhibited immense influence over the other young people in the group. I could have easily judged this young man for being a troublemaker, but in fact he turned out to be my greatest ally whilst delivering my workshops. He arrived before the start the workshop every day, was always ready to answer any questions I asked, fully took part in any exercise I set and even made sure the other young people did not disturb me or show disrespect whilst I was presenting! During the last workshop of that particular programme, he shared his story and his WHY.

He told the group that he grew up with a best friend that was like a little brother to him. This friend had never been in trouble with the law, he was a good person who was smart and did well in school. He, on the on the other hand had started a life of crime, fully involved with gang culture and selling crack cocaine and at the age of nineteen he became a cocaine addict. Despite their differing lifestyles, they shared a very strong childhood bond. One day this young man gave a lift to his best friend, who is seventeen years old and they were involved in a horrific car accident, he escaped the crash with minor injuries and whiplash, his best friend was killed instantly. The question he asked himself was, WHY did I live and he died? I have done all this wrong in my life and God saved me and took him! WHY? The guilt and remorse that he felt was his fuel to turn his life around. His energy and motivation to overcome his addiction to drugs came from this tragic incident and now he is one of the most motivated, positive and enthusiastic individuals I have ever met!

29

It was clear that this young man's WHY in life was clear, the memories and remorse confronted him every day and it provided him with the passion and the determination to better himself. Great leaders, great businesses, great organizations and great relationships do not forget their WHY. The heartbeat and the source of energy is the WHY.

Similarly, it is just as easy for two people to sometimes get lost within a marriage; they drift apart and forget the love and the ideals with which they embarked on their journey together and before they realise it they have become strangers! A successful marriage involves falling in love many times but always with the same person. In the same way leaders have to consistently communicate the WHY of what they are doing to keep the flame of motivation and productivity alive in their people. Large multinational corporations that become fixated on numbers and bottom line results and forget their WHY, are like forgetful dinosaurs on their way to extinction! It is the leadership that must infuse the WHY into every aspect of the corporate culture to keep the organization and its people alive and vibrant.

Leadership as an Adventure

So WHY are you a leader? And what exactly is leadership? Many writers, thinkers and social scientists have given some really insightful definitions and theories of leadership. I would like to share with you my definition of leadership and also my WHY for the work I do. To put it very simply I would say leadership is an adventure, hence the title for this book!

Let's take a closer look at these two words; the Oxford Dictionary defines the word '*leadership*' as:

'*The action of leading a group of people or an organization.*'

and defines the word '*adventure*' as:

'*An unusual and exciting or daring experience.*'

Leading others really does bring you face to face with lots of unusual, exciting and daring experiences! Great adventures and great leadership requires bravery and one of the bravest things a leader can do is look at themselves with honesty and constantly seek to improve themselves.

The great intrinsic benefits of embarking on any adventure is what you learn about yourself in the process. As an ancient Chinese proverb says:

'To know others, one must first know oneself.'

My personal WHY behind the work I do and this book is primarily because of what I have learnt about myself, what I have had to change, and will continue to change about myself, and who I have to become within myself along the journey. Sometimes leadership is portrayed or defined as an act that changes or transforms others, which of course is true, but I would say the act of leadership is even more transformational for the leader themselves, if they are willing to learn from their experience and be open to change.

It's over to you now to reflect on your WHY and note down some of your ideas in this first part of our adventure together…

Summary Key Points & Self Reflection:

1. Can you explain your own personal WHY for doing what you do?

   _____

   _____

   _____

   _____

2. In one sentence write down your own WHY.

   _____

   _____

   _____

   _____

3. How can you connect your team to the WHY?

_____

_____

_____

_____

4. What are you going to do differently to connect people to the organizational WHY and understand their individual WHY?

_____

_____

_____

_____

5. Commit to 3 things that you are going to do from today to harness the power of WHY?

_____

_____

_____

_____

Notes

_____

_____

_____

_____

_____

_____

_____

_____

_____

_____

_____

_____

_____

_____

_____

_____

Chapter 2

THE POWER OF EMOTIONS

We like to think of ourselves as rational people, rationality being seen as a good quality to develop. A rational person is often perceived as objective, fair and trustworthy, but on the other hand, if you were to describe someone as being emotional, what sort of a person comes to mind? Someone who cannot think clearly, who is unstable and could fly off the handle in a fit of anger, or break down in a flood of tears at any moment. We strive to bring rationality into education and business, we try to raise our children to be rational and we like to think, that as ourselves, we make rational decisions.

However, the fact still remains that human beings are emotional animals rather than rational ones. Take a moment to consider the most important decisions you have made during your life so far; have they been based more on your feelings and emotions rather than rationality? Did you decide to get married too quickly or fall in love based on a rational analysis of all the pros and cons? The unforgettable moment you first held your new born baby in your arms is not a moment of rationality, but rather one of pure emotion; or when somebody close to you passes away, is it rational thoughts or emotional feelings you experience? Your most profound and intense experiences of being alive and conscious are filled with emotion and emotions are very powerful feelings. A great leader recognises the power of emotions, they understand how to harness their powers and channel them into motivation and productivity.

Emotions are fuel. The emotions of anger, excitement, jealousy, love, gratitude, joy, hatred and all the other feelings we as human beings experience at various times in our life, can move us towards actions, they can fuel our behaviour. Even emotions like sadness and depression can be used as fuel for taking action.

For example, a person who is very sad or negative about life, who does not want to get out of bed, who does not want to see or engage with the outside world in anyway. He has resolved in his mind to confine himself to his bedroom and feel sorry for himself. His best friend comes to visit him, he tries his best to console him, tries to convince him to take a walk outside and enjoy the sunshine, but nothing seems to work and so this friend tries a different strategy. He starts saying things that will really annoy the sad friend! The best friend starts to make his depressed friend feel angry, so the best friend continues and now, instead of feeling depressed, he feels furious, to such an extent that he jumps out of bed and punches his best friend on the nose!

What just happened in this scenario? Feelings of sadness were transformed into feelings of anger and the result was action. The best friend may not have expected to get punched but at least he was successful at getting his friend out of bed and changing his emotional state. Sadness changed into anger, but also let's consider that they both end up laughing about it, again there is another change, sadness changed to anger and anger changed to laughter! I am not suggesting for a moment that leaders in a professional capacity in their business or organization, should annoy their team members and colleagues so much that they are driven to assault them, but I am trying to convey the idea that skilful leaders are able to harness and transform the emotions of the people they lead so that they are moved towards taking the actions that the leader needs them to take. In this case the best friend was successful in achieving his aim of getting his friend out of bed.

Toxic Teams

Leadership can be likened to a game of chess, where the leader has to think strategically before making a move. A good chess player knows not only how each piece moves, but also when and how to use each piece to ultimately win the game. The great leader knows their people, they know the emotional state of each member of their team and they know how and when to strategically engage and transform the emotions of their people, to awaken their interest, ignite their passion, create excitement and motivate them to achieve and deliver on a specific result. There is a big difference between emotional manipulation and strategically influencing other people's emotions, for their own good and for the wider environment.

When a leader manipulates the emotions of the people, they create a poisonous toxic environment that is not only unproductive, but can damage the reputation and, ultimately, the very existence of the organization or business. Toxic leaders create toxic teams through stirring up people's emotions to create an environment of negativity, mistrust and suspicion. These types of manipulative leaders, use the emotion of fear to control their people. If you believed that your supervisor or manager would not think twice about dismissing you if you made the slightest mistake, if you knew that your leader would willingly deceive you without a second's thought, if it served their own interests, then how motivated would you be to bring your best mood and abilities to your work? Would you want to be innovative and bring new ideas forward? How much loyalty and commitment would you have to the business or organization?

A culture of fear and mistrust is not a healthy environment for productivity, motivation, innovation or loyalty! Leaders shape the culture of an organization, business or team for better or worse. Parents as the leaders of their family, can influence their children in a positive or negative way, just as the teacher in the classroom sets the tone for the behaviour of their class. Leaders can have a massive influence over the actions and behaviours of the people they lead and they do this primarily by the emotions they are able to create in other people. A team where unhealthy internal competition, backbiting, gossiping, lying and other negative behaviours is the norm, is often led by a leader that has allowed, either consciously or unconsciously, for those negative emotions and behaviours to fester. The stereotypical tyrannical leader is an emotional manipulator who primarily runs his affairs through fear and that can never be a good leadership trait for a country, an organization, a classroom or a family.

Great leaders are not emotional manipulators but rather they are strategic, conscious influencers of emotions in order to provide a positive outcome or result. On the whole, they seek to create positive emotions in the people they lead, emotions such as pride and joy; emotions that are created when people feel like they are valued and acknowledged for their contributions. Great leaders establish a culture where people feel secure, create an environment in which innovation is encouraged, everyone safe in the knowledge that mistakes are not the end of the world. At times, even the greatest leaders can create emotions of anger, frustration or fear in others, however, it is always with a bigger strategy in mind to achieve a specific positive outcome or result, not just as the modus operandi of every day. Great leaders understand the immense power of creating strong positive emotions and feelings in the people that they lead.

Engagement and Play

Babies are amazing tiny humans able to fully express their emotions; if they are upset about something they cry and if they are in the mood to play and giggle they will do so completely naturally. A game of 'peek a boo' is all it takes to get them to smile or laugh hysterically. With toddlers and young children, being at play is a natural thing kids do, so why is it that as we grow up, we stop playing? A smile or a laugh does not flow as naturally as it did when we were children; does society expect us to become serious, mature and boring? Some of the most outstanding and inspirational leaders and teachers in the world are some of the most playful characters you will ever meet. They have retained that special childhood playfulness, creativity and imagination and these qualities do wonders for the workplace, for organizations, teams and families.

'Work hard, play hard' is a maxim we have heard many times, but there does not necessarily have to be a separation between work and play. Great leaders make work into play, they use humour and fun to really get the best out of their people. Disengaged employees leave organizations and businesses, in many cases because their job does not offer challenge or satisfaction - to put it in another way, their job is boring and their manager or supervisor is dreary and lacks inspiration and leadership! As a leader, you can powerfully impact the emotions of the people you lead if you can bring playfulness and fun into your leadership approach, your people will be more motivated and more productive as a result. A light hearted, fun work environment or home life does not mean that serious work and serious discussions do not take place. The idea is not that the workplace or business is run like a circus and the leader has to provide the fun and entertainment like a clown, but more so that great leaders know, deep down, that everyone is a child at heart and at times, play and engagement is a very powerful strategy to implement, to utilise their people's skills and abilities.

The business world is stressful and so is family life at times. In our fast paced, technologically advanced modern world, which is supposed to make our life easier, things are becoming more and more complicated. Stress, and stress related illnesses, are on the increase. In our digital age our relationships are strained, they lack depth and meaning, our social media has turned us into extremely unsocial beings as everyone has a smartphone, but we seem to be becoming thoughtless and nonsensical as no one really seems to talk or listen to each other!

"I fear the day that technology will surpass our human interaction. The world will have a generation of idiots."

Albert Einstein

Our mental wellbeing is at stake and leaders that harness the power of play and laughter, help to lessen the burden of stress. If you can use humour at times of pressure in your life, it does wonders for your health and lightens the load for those that look to you for leadership. Play and humour increases the serotonin levels in our body, so we experience positive feelings and we can be more creative. The leader that strategically uses the power of play and fun can also give feedback to their people in a way that they are not offended, but still receive the message. Play and fun foster innovation and creativity, which are great for business.

As a leader, are you an energy booster or an energy zapper? In some computer games, especially the retro ones such as Sonic the Hedgehog, Mario Brothers and Pacman, there are elements to these games which increase your energy levels and there are events that use up your energy and zap you! In the same way with life, you will have people you know that can increase your energy levels and make you feel better, but on the flip side, you will know people who can bring you down and make you feel depressed, when you were in a pretty good mood – energy zappers! As a leader you can transmit positive or negative energy to your people. If you boost people through play and engagement they feel good, if they feel good they are likely to transmit that good feeling to your customers and clients. To implement a culture of play and engagement in your workplace or your business, you do not need to try and imitate the Google offices and have slides or keep space hoppers for chairs! However, it is important as a leader that you have a positive energy and are able to connect with your inner child when needed.

Brain Wiring

This book aims to make you a better leader by raising your awareness. You will have a better understanding of both yourself and your people, because we are all wired biologically in very similar ways.

We as human beings have more in common with each other than the differences that sometimes divide us. It is a fact that all human DNA is pretty much identical, around 99.9% of all human DNA is the same, only 0.1% makes up the differences such as your colour and race. If we have more in common with each other as human beings, then why do we focus so much on our differences? The truly great leaders acknowledge differences and yet unite diversely different people towards a common goal and purpose. If you want to really harness the power of emotions to motivate your people and get the best out of them, then as a leader, having a basic understanding of how the human brain works will be immensely beneficial to you, especially when dealing with emotional storms.

We have a rational and an emotional brain, these parts of the brain being interconnected through an extremely complex and intricate system of neural networks. What are emotions from a purely biological perspective? Neuro-chemicals in the brain that make us feel certain feelings. The prefrontal cortex of the brain allows us to rationalise and assess situations, while the emotional brain, or limbic system, is the part of the brain that is responsible for our emotions. Within the limbic system, the amygdala is the main trigger point for emotions in the brain. If it perceives a threat it can send powerful signals to the adrenal glands which trigger a release of hormones preparing the body for action, this trigger is commonly known as the fight or flight response.

Imagine a caveman or cavewoman faced with a terrifying stampede of huge tusked woolly mammoths charging towards them! Their body would trigger a response that prepares them for action, a burst of energy that allows them to fight or take flight and run for their lives. This survival mechanism and response to stress has been with us since prehistoric times and is still with us in our modern lives, only the chances of us needing to escape wild animals or fight life threatening duels is rare. However, your body does not make a distinction between a real life-threatening situation and many of our modern day woolly mammoths take the form of traffic jams, public speaking, marital disputes, financial pressures, disputes, confrontations and work deadlines, or even the tone of an email can trigger your own or somebody else's fight or flight response.

The list of our modern-day stressors is endless and seems to be increasing! For the leader this awareness is very important. An unaware or simply poor leader can trigger a negative emotional response in their people without realising it and the amygdala of a colleague or team member can be triggered into fight or flight to the point where they are ready to throttle the boss to death! However, the prefrontal cortex of the brain can override the initial emotional response of the amygdala and so ensures that the colleague or team member's response is more reasonable, otherwise the amygdala's response would be acted upon, which wouldn't be good news for the boss! At times of emergency, the emotional brain can override the rational thinking parts of the brain and at other times, the rational part of our brain can override our initial emotional response. A great leader is aware of what emotional response they are triggering in other people, they are tuned in.

Tuning In

Generally speaking, hysterical laughing and cracking loud jokes is not expected behaviour when attending somebody's funeral, just as trembling with fear would not look good to the guests on your wedding day. As a leader, if you are not aware of the emotions felt by the people you lead, it can be very difficult to motivate them and utilise their best efforts. A leader triggers the appropriate emotions in other people to move them towards the outcomes and results that are required. The emotional state of the leader has to be in tune with the emotional state of the people they lead and the external circumstances. The leader's ability to attune themselves to others is the foundation upon which emotionally intelligent leadership is built. A great leader is aware of the thoughts, feelings, emotions and moods of the group or team so they can lead them better.

•

Emotions travel, they move, they are transmitted and they are contagious. Emotions can travel at lightning speed. Have you ever seen the fans at a football match or the spectators at a boxing match, where you can see the passion, excitement and euphoria engulf the crowd? A major tragic event reported in the media can set off a feeling of national grief across the country. The leader is the vessel to capture and reflect the group's emotions but more importantly, their duty is to channel that emotion into a positive direction. The president or prime minister of a country that has suffered a major terrorist attack, who sheds a tear or looks visibly upset as they address the nation on television, reflects the emotion of everyone watching. The importance of the leader's tear is a vital acknowledgment of what has happened, it allows people to express their feelings of grief regarding the tragedy but the leader's job does not end there. The president cannot just break down in tears, they must say the words and express the feelings that bring the nation together and move them courageously forward.

EMOTIONS TRAVEL

I regularly coach senior executives and leaders in large multinational corporations and occasionally I come across two types of leaders: the first is the leader that just does not care about the emotions of team members or colleagues, they do not care how they are perceived by others and are completely out of tune with the collective emotions of the team or department; the second type of leader is one who is in denial, this type of leader wants to ignore the uncomfortable emotions of the group or team and pretend they do not exist. Senior management decisions, major upheaval such as restructuring and mergers, change, pressure, stress and deadlines, all have an emotional impact on the group. If the leader chooses to ignore how people feel about matters, it can start to breed an environment of negativity and result in a toxic unproductive team. Leaders that suffer from the ostrich syndrome try to bury their heads in the sand, hoping to ignore the combination of emotions in the workplace, but who usually set themselves up for bigger problems down the line.

Tuning into others means raising your awareness as a leader regarding the emotional pulse of your people. The self-absorbed leader who is only interested in facts, figures, logic and rationality, does not understand that no matter how much we try to apply reason, analysis and logic to our working lives, the invisible world of emotions has a funny way of impacting almost everything we do. You have to spend one-to-one coaching time with your people to find out what is on their mind; find out how they feel about certain situations. As a leader you have to have your eyes and ears on the ground. It is your job to take an active interest in the emotions your people may feel about their work or their role and you have to anticipate and look out for warning signals that tell you the group or team is not happy. Being on the lookout for signals and warnings that something is not right within the emotional tone of your people, means that as a leader you can avert issues before they happen.

Emotionally Intelligent Leaders

Intellectual and analytical ability alone does not make a great leader; indeed, the heart of leadership is the leadership of the heart, not just the head. Inspiring purpose, igniting passion and infusing playfulness into a team, provides the framework for the engaging leader's emotional toolkit. A leader with only a sledgehammer in his toolkit will eventually smash the spirit of a team, resulting in poor performance and low productivity. A good experienced golfer develops a feel for which club he should use and how he should approach the particular challenge of each shot, depending upon the terrain of the golf course, and he chooses the most appropriate tool for the job. An emotionally intelligent leader understands and develops a feel for which particular leadership style will maximise people's abilities and will constantly drive positive feelings in those they lead.

Psychologist and bestselling author of *'Emotional Intelligence'*, Daniel Goldman, has carried out research into the areas of Emotional Intelligence and Leadership and has identified six distinct leadership styles:

- Coaching Leadership
- Visionary Leadership
- Affiliative Leadership
- Democratic Leadership
- Pacesetting Leadership
- Commanding Leadership

VISIONARY

COACHING

AFFILIATIVE

DEMOCRATIC

PACE-SETTING

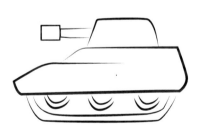

COMMANDING

A coaching approach to leadership is all about having one-to-one meetings with team members, it is about matching individual goals with organizational ones and really finding out what makes people tick. The key to using a coaching approach is asking the right questions and listening carefully to the answers. The visionary leader is one that uses their words powerfully to grow people's excitement about a future goal, they cast an optimistic vision of the future that keep people motivated and striving towards the vision. The visionary leader connects with people's shared aspirations and hopes for the future.

When Dr Martin Luther King said the words,

'. . .I have a dream. . .',

he made a visionary and inspirational call for racial equality and an end to discrimination. What is the future vision you would like your people to become excited about?

The affiliative leader creates strong bonds and relationships, this type of leader is one that is able to create a friendly and caring atmosphere, this can be very useful at times of stress or navigating through conflicts. The democratic leader is one that places high value on other people's input and participation, this type of leader makes people feel that they are part of the process and that their suggestions and ideas matter, people feel engaged and listened to.

The democratic approach to leadership is very useful for creativity, generating ideas and obtaining valuable suggestions, just by simply asking the question of your team, 'what do you think?' Or, 'what are your suggestions and ideas on how we should approach this?' A word of warning however, when asking for another person's input, is to only ask if you genuinely want to listen to them. People can sense when a leader is asking only for the sake of it and has already decided the course of action in their mind anyway, this can be very disengaging and in which case it is better not to use the democratic approach. Asking for people's opinions and suggestions does not mean you, as the leader, have to agree or implement their ideas, however, as a leader if you ask for input from your team, you should be prepared to genuinely listen.

The pacesetting leader sets high standards and targets. This style of leadership is one in which the leader pushes the team along to hit deadlines and produce work of good quality. It is the no nonsense, '*let's get down to business*' approach to leadership, which is assertive and clear, but not aggressive. The pacesetting leadership style can be very useful for motivating an experienced and competent team, especially if the leader has also combined their pacesetting approach with an affiliative one. In this situation the leader can push the team along when needed and no one takes offence, as they realise that the leader cares about them and they have created strong bonds, which can withstand the strains of pressures and deadlines. The pacesetting approach can be de-motivating if executed poorly.

The commanding approach to leadership is very clear and very direct and can be useful when dealing with emergencies and serious problems. This style of leadership is where the leader may raise their voice or demonstrate other types of behaviour that could be viewed as aggressive, however the situation is so serious that it justifies a commanding approach. It is a sad fact of the business world and our working lives that many leaders and managers perpetually use a commanding leadership style to strike fear into the hearts of the people they lead. These types of leaders use a sledgehammer to crack a nut all the time and it really does great damage to the morale and ultimately the longevity of the team. For you to become a powerful, emotionally, intelligent leader and really get the most out of your people you have to know which style of leadership to use and when, maybe combining styles to suite the situation and when to change leadership styles, just as with golf or chess when you have to adapt and use the appropriate tool or move for the situation.

Receiving Feedback as a Leader

Many people have the false view that leadership is about exercising power over others, about being the one in charge who is able to control everything and everyone around them. Many leaders may believe that as a leader, they are entitled to perks and benefits, the big office, the best parking spot and keeping which ever workings hours they wish, however, really effective powerful leaders know that leadership is not a bed of roses, it's hard work! The mere fact that you are in a leadership position opens you up to be judged. Leaders will be criticised and judged either overtly or discreetly behind their backs. It is better for you as a leader to know what your people really think and feel about you, however to face this might be tough, you may hear some things that you don't like. How you respond to feedback, criticism, judgement and negativity is what will set you apart a leader.

'*Mirror, mirror on the wall, who's the fairest leader of them all?*' We all love to be praised and admired for our personal traits and achievements, in fact when somebody sings our praises, it's as if our ears double in size as we stand basking in the praise, pretending to be humble! What is our response when somebody points out our faults and criticises us? Our response in these situations is the difference between being an average leader and being a truly great one. Is all criticism bad? Criticism is just feedback and this type of feedback can be of two types: firstly, negative feedback, which you feel is untrue and unfair and, secondly, negative feedback which you know deep down is true. For example, imagine you receive some honest feedback from your team members in that they believe you are a little bit of a hypocrite, they feel that what you say and what you do are two different things - they find it hard to trust you. If you feel this is completely unfair and untrue, you should still not respond defensively, great leaders do not take offense to criticism, even if they feel it is unfounded.

A great leader responds to negative criticism like a scientist conducting an experiment. The scientist is objectively trying to get to the bottom of whatever problem they are trying to solve and has the ability of mind to research, explore, and test the hypothesis. In a similar way, as a leader, you should respond to negative feedback objectively to see whether or not what the team are saying is true. The fact that your team members believe you are a hypocrite and that your words and actions do not match up, may or may not be true, despite how you feel about it. It could be that the team has a false perception of you in which case it is your job as the leader to investigate where this false perception stems from, it's got into their heads from somewhere! If, however, after some honest and objective introspection you realise that the criticism has truth to it, then you need to face up to it, not respond in an emotional way; do everything in your power to change yourself and take action on the feedback. It can be tough accepting criticism but if you take it on board and work on yourself, your positive response alone could be enough to start to change your team's perceptions of you and if you actually take the steps to change your negative behaviour, it will positively impact your team and be massively rewarding for you personally.

Life is a school and learning never comes to an end, life can teach us many lessons - some can be extremely difficult, but also positively transformative if we learn and grow from them. Leadership is also a massive learning experience, do not approach leadership with 'a *know it all*' attitude. If, as a leader, you have the spirit of learning in your heart, it will truly serve you well. To be a great leader you will need to develop the inner resources to take on feedback and criticism, you cannot respond in an emotional and sensitive way. You may have to face some painful truths about yourself along your leadership journey and you may have to face your own weaknesses and look them face to face in the mirror of truth. Finally, as a leader, you will have to develop your self-awareness and your self-mastery to control your emotions and discipline yourself to develop powerful positive habits. The power of self-mastery is the next chapter which we will explore in more detail but before that, take some time to reflect on what you have learnt from this chapter and the Power of Emotions.

Summary Key Points & Self Reflection

1. Think of a time when you have transmitted and received a positive emotion? What was the emotion and how did it make you feel?

   _____

   _____

   _____

   _____

2. Think of a time when you have transmitted and received a negative emotion. What was the emotion and how did it make you feel?

   _____

   _____

   _____

   _____

3. How aware are you of your own negative emotions or thoughts? What signals alert you to these negative emotions?

_____

_____

_____

_____

4. To what extent do your emotions impact your relationships and performance at work? How does your behaviour change?

_____

_____

_____

_____

5. What are you going to do proactively to seek feedback or become more self-aware?

_____

_____

_____

_____

6. List some of inner resources you have or need to develop further to be honest about your areas of improvement.

_____

_____

_____

_____

Notes

Chapter 3

THE POWER OF
SELF-MASTERY

There are many ancient tales and legends surrounding the Japanese Samurai Warriors. It was said that duels between two warriors were sometimes decided without either warrior ever needing to draw their sword, or engage in combat. Two warriors would meet and stand face to face, they would look into each other's eyes, no words would be exchanged and after some time, one man would step away, bow and accept defeat. The eyes are the window to the soul and it is said that the warriors were looking into each other's spirit to see who had a stronger fighting spirit, who had trained harder and who was more determined, all of this would simply be seen in a warrior's eyes. The legendary boxer Muhammed Ali, used to say that the outcome of a fight was not decided inside the ring on the day of the boxing match, but on the lonely early morning runs and intense training sessions that no one sees. To truly be a great leader you have to train hard to master your own emotions, thoughts, and habits before you can lead others. As the Chinese General Sun Tzu has said . . .

'The man who masters himself, master's others. . .'

SELF-MASTERY

We have heard of the children's game *'Follow the Leader'*, but have you ever asked yourself, as a leader, whether you are worth following? Or, to put it another way, why should others follow you or listen to what you have to say? We all have people in our lives that we look up to and respect, those people have certain traits and characteristics that we admire. Just as you admire certain things about other people, you have a duty as a leader to develop traits within your character and within your life that other people find admirable, inspirational, and respectful. As a leader one of your most important priorities is to constantly work on yourself, which means to constantly seek to remove faulty thinking and negative habits from your life and imbed positive, empowering thoughts and habits into your daily life, so that they become part of your personality and who you are. The leader has to hold his or herself to a higher standard of behaviour, which is what earns them the respect and admiration of the people they lead. People are willing to listen and follow a leader who has mastered themselves. The greatest leaders are dedicated to mastering their thoughts, words, and actions, they are dedicated to constant growth.

In the corporate world, in organizations of all sizes and in our schools and families, we are facing a leadership crisis. Leaders that cannot be trusted. These leaders say one thing, but think something completely different in their minds and do something altogether different through their actions. They are leaders that do not practice what they preach, leaders that feel they are above the rules and leaders that are incongruent. The mentality of many leaders is one of pure selfishness, where lining their own pockets and serving their own interests is the only thing that matters! They have no empathy or care for their people, they have never been down in the trenches with the team to really understand what matters from the ground up and they seek to lord over all from their ivory tower. These types of leaders blame their employees, their students and their children and constantly point out their faults, it never crosses their mind to look within to change something about themselves and their approach as a starting point. Great leaders look within and master themselves first.

Leadership requires a great deal of energy. When you dedicate yourself as a leader to the cultivation of your energy, through developing self-awareness and self-discipline, you gain insights about yourself that allow you to lead better. Business and family life can be very stressful at times and leaders can find themselves under immense pressure. How will you, as a leader, stay sane, think clearly and make the right decisions when a situation becomes really intense within your personal and professional life? One of your greatest allies at times like this will be your personal disciplines. The powerful and positive thinking patterns you have trained your mind to think about and the daily personal habits that you have trained yourself to implement. Self-mastery will transform you into a very powerful and effective leader and it all begins in the mind.

Choose Your Thoughts

Sam worked for a fishmonger in San Francisco and his job was to take the fish from the factory and load the freezer truck. One day, towards the end of his shift, Sam was loading the truck when he found that the doors of the freezer truck had shut in on themselves - Sam found himself trapped in the dark inside the freezer truck. He tried as hard as he could to open the doors but they wouldn't budge and he tried shouting to his workmates at the top of his voice, but they did not hear him, as most of them had already gone home for the day. It was then that Sam began to panic, his thoughts took over, he calculated the temperature of the freezer and came to the conclusion that he was going to spend the night in the freezing temperatures and freeze to death. This one thought took over his mind - I am going to freeze to death, I am going to freeze to death.

The next morning his workmates opened the doors of the truck to find Sam's dead body. The autopsy revealed he had died from frost bite, so they checked the temperature of the freezer in the truck and to their amazement, they discovered that the freezer had been switched off, Sam had not been trapped in a freezing environment at all! So, what killed him? His thoughts and his belief that he was going to freeze! Our thoughts are very powerful. There is a mind-body connection that no leader can afford to ignore. In Sam's case his fear of freezing had caused his body to manifest the physical symptoms of frost bite. Your thoughts can have a massive impact on your physical and mental wellbeing so you must train your mind to think positive, wholesome and helpful thoughts.

Everything begins in the mind; the starting point of all things is one's thoughts. The Irish play-wright, George Bernard Shaw, once said:

'You are the window from which you view the world'

How do you, as a leader see the world? How do you see yourself? And, how do you see others? The answers to these questions will depend on what paradigms you hold in your mind. A paradigm is simply the lens through which you interpret things. Our paradigms or lens is made up of many things, such as our upbringing, our culture, our values, beliefs and experiences. Looking at a glass of water filled half way, the optimist may say it's a glass half full, great! And the pessimist may look at the same glass of water and say it's a glass that is half empty, oh dear! The glass of water can be seen in both ways, a glass half full or a glass half empty, but a person's mental paradigm determines what they see and how they interpret events. It is vitally important for leaders to develop positive and empowering paradigms and ways of interpreting events. Fear, doubt and negative thoughts are not the thinking patterns of great leaders.

Great leaders CHOOSE their thoughts. Most people have very reactive thinking patterns, if something does not go according to plan or goes wrong then that event is bad, if something goes the way we want it to go, then that event is good. Good and bad are the labels we give to the things that happen to us in our lives, truly great leaders have trained their mind to go beyond their knee jerk reactions to external events. Even the greatest leaders may still feel an initial negative thought, but very quickly they become aware of their thoughts and stop it, they then CHOOSE to interpret that thought in a way that is useful and productive. For many of us, interpreting events in a negative way and thinking negative thoughts, feels natural because we have been doing it for most of our lives, but if you really want to powerfully motivate others and get the best of them, you must begin by training your own mind to think positively, firstly by reframing negative thoughts.

Three steps to reframing negative thoughts.

1. Become aware of your negative thoughts and thinking patterns.

2. Challenge the basis of your negative thoughts.

3. CHOOSE to interpret events with positive and productive thoughts.

Everything in this world is created twice! What does this mean? Everything is thought about in somebody's mind first and then it is created and brought out into the physical world. The clothes you are wearing, the furniture in your home and the buildings you see around you, all began as thoughts in somebody's mind first and then they were created in the physical world. As leaders, we have to be very aware and careful about the thoughts that we think, because sooner or later our thoughts will manifest themselves into our physical reality. For example, if you have a real deep dislike of somebody, but do not want them to know what you really think about them, your feelings of dislike towards that person will sooner or later manifest itself in large or small ways, in the way in which you interact with them. If we try to suppress our thoughts and feelings it can be very unhealthy for us, the bottom line is our thoughts as the leader in the work environment or in our family situations will come out. Let's make sure our thoughts take us and others in the right direction. Our thoughts can take us in a negative downward spiral or they can take us in an upward positive spiral…

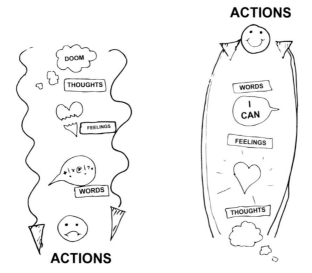

Choose Your Words

The thoughts we think are powerful, but it could be argued that our words are even more powerful than our thoughts. Do our thoughts shape our words or do the words that we speak actually shape our thoughts and paradigms? This is an interesting question and an entire field of study has been developed around it, popularly known as NLP, which stands for neuro-linguistic programming, exploring how our brains can be re-programmed based on the words we speak and the type of language we use. Try this quick challenge, no matter what you do, DO NOT THINK ABOUT A YELLOW RHINO! When you read that sentence, what was one of the first thoughts that crossed your mind? It was probably a yellow rhino because to understand the instructions you are forced to think of the yellow rhino to then try and stop thinking about the yellow rhino! Leaders have to be aware of the words they use and choose their words carefully so as to really get the best results out of themselves and the people they lead.

Winston Churchill's speeches during World War II are famous for their strength and determination, particularly when he said:

'We shall fight on the beaches...we shall never, never, never give up!'

These were powerful, encouraging words, they acted as a powerful rallying call to consolidate and bolster the morale of the British for the war effort. At times of immense pressure or stress, it is crucial that you, as a leader, use the right words to show that you are a source of strength, a rock amongst a sea of chaos. At times of great sorrow and grief you must use words that show your compassion and empathy. Leaders that use the right words at the right time, establish a connection with people. In your day to day interactions with people, start to become aware of the words that you use on a regular basis. Do you as a leader use words such as, I think, I can't, not sure, I doubt, or even non-words like 'err' regularly? Become aware of the potential impact your words might have on your own feelings and what feelings your words might be creating in those around you. Great leaders speak with purpose; they use their words as a tool to move people in the direction they want. Just as you must train yourself to choose your thoughts, you must also train yourself to choose your words. Words really can make or break a leader.

DO NOT USE = REPLACE WITH:

Problem = CHALLENGE
Manageable = ACHIEVABLE
I think = I BELIEVE

What if the leader speaks negative and discouraging words? What if the leader's words are full of doubt, fear and mistrust? The rhyme, 'sticks and stones may break my bones but words will never hurt me', does not apply to leadership. The negative words of the leader can create feelings of doubt, fear and mistrust in the team and can be the ultimate undoing of the leader. Stress and stress-related illnesses are on the increase and one of the biggest stressors in the workplace is a bad manager. Often these types of leaders use harsh and cutting words to their employees or colleagues, they may be sarcastic or just simply rude and the words may not even be spoken, it could be written in an email or a text message but this type of communication has a disastrous effect on the team morale and long-term productivity. Leaders may try to threaten and manipulate the people they lead through words that create fear and anxiety, but they are really damaging the outcome of the work that needs to be produced and its quality.

When a leader speaks words that are positive and encouraging it does wonders for a team. The power of acknowledgement cannot be underestimated and you should think about how you can implement more genuine acknowledgements and praise into your leadership approach. We all like to be recognized for our achievements and an acknowledgement with a few words, either verbal or written, is a boost of positive energy that can create feelings of pride and satisfaction within your people. Some leaders like to be miserly about giving praise or acknowledgement and others go overboard, dishing it out all the time so it comes across as fake and holds little value. A powerful and great leader knows that their words carry weight, they know when and how to praise and acknowledge, and they use their words to drive positive feelings within the people they lead to motivate them to greater levels of productivity and output.

Actions, Behaviours and Habits

Mastering your thoughts and words are an important part of you becoming a more effective and powerful leader. The act of changing how you think and how you speak should also translate positively into your actions, external behaviour and personal habits. Your brain is flexible, it is malleable and it can change and adapt, the technical term for this ability is known as neuroplasticity. Your brain is made up of millions of neurons all firing different signals to each other in a vast complicated and intricate system. Your habits can be seen from a biological view point as patterns of neurons in the brain, one neuron sends an electrical signal to another neuron and this connection is known as a synapse. It is possible to create new neural connections and new synapses in the brain; therefore, you are able to create new habits and behaviours. Our brains are made for change, adaptation and learning, it is up to us as leaders whether or not we take advantage of this great gift of nature to put in the effort to change our habits and behaviours.

Successful people have successful habits, if you want to be a successful individual and a successful leader you must examine your personal habits, look squarely into the often-painful mirror of truth, and root out all the habits and behaviours that are holding you back. Negative thinking patterns and unhelpful emotional responses can be changed through effort and awareness. Physical habits can be reprogrammed so, for example, if you are a lazy person or you have the tendency to procrastinate and delay tasks, you can implement new habits into your life to combat your laziness and procrastination. Often leaders know the truth in what it is about their behaviour that is holding them back, why they have not yet achieved their goals or fulfilled their true potential. The real question is, are you willing to do what it takes to change your habits and behaviours?

We live in a world of instant gratification, everything we want - right here, right now! Why wait? You don't have to wait to save up money to buy your dream home or car, just take out a loan or a credit card now and do not worry about the future. You do not need to wait and put in effort at the gym to have your perfect waistline, just undertake this quick medical procedure and wham, you've got it now! We demand instant meals and instant relationships in a world full of smart phones with thoughtless and senseless people, social media rants and anti-social humans! However, despite our mad craving for instant results, to implement real lasting change within ourselves is not a quick fix. It is said that to create the beginnings of a new neural pathway in our brains takes at least thirty days of consistent action. For example, if you want to programme your mind to wake up early every day at 5.45am, then you need to wake up every day at 5.45am for at least thirty days to create the brain connection for the new habit. Real change takes time and effort, this is nature's way but if you can stick to it through all the temptations and when things get tough, then you will have mastered yourself and will emerge as a great leader.

There was an occasion when a zookeeper tried an experiment on three different types of monkeys: a gorilla, a chimpanzee and a bonobo. The zookeeper threw a key into the cage with the gorilla but the gorilla took no notice. He was too busy eating and did not show any response to the key whatsoever. The zookeeper then threw a key into the cage with the chimpanzee and the chimpanzee did respond to the key, he was interested and picked it up, started digging with it and banged it on the bars of the cage, there was definitely some response. Lastly, the zookeeper threw a key into the cage with the bonobo and within twenty minutes the bonobo had picked up the key, worked out how to use the key, unlocked the cage and set himself free. What type of monkey are you? Are you someone that is not bothered about your personal development as a leader like the gorilla; are you going to try to implement some of the principles in this book but give up when things get tough, a bit like the chimpanzee; or are you like the bonobo who takes immediate action and begins to implement change without hesitation. The choice is of course yours, but great leaders implement great ideas quickly - they take action.

Being Your Best Every Day

Mastering your thoughts, words and actions will be hard work but it will transform you into a highly effective and congruent individual, you will become the type of person that other people will trust and want to follow. Great leaders bring the best of themselves to any given situation every day. We all have within us the worst version of ourselves and also the best version, but it is absolutely 100% our choice which version of ourselves we aim to be. Mastering yourself is a powerful leadership secret because not many leaders see it as a focus area, they are too concerned with how to master and control others. If you understand clearly that discipline is your friend, not your enemy, then you will have the commitment to do what it takes to work on yourself daily. Leaders need to earn their self-worth on a daily basis and self-worth can only be earned by disciplining yourself to do the right thing daily.

People who, deep down, do not actually like themselves very much, can cause a lot of problems for themselves and those around them. Low self-esteem or low self-worth can stem from a variety of reasons, but a common one is where an individual keeps on breaking their own commitments and promises they make to themselves. If you say you are going to do something make sure you do it because, over time, if you keep saying you will do things, but you fail to, you begin to erode the trust in yourself and if you do not have trust in yourself, how can you ever expect to be effective as a leader? One of my first martial arts teachers once said that you cannot make peace somewhere else, unless you are at peace with yourself first. Leadership starts with you leading yourself first. Leaders with high self-worth and esteem are leaders that always make the right decisions, they are comfortable with making unpopular decisions. If, by sticking to their principles and doing what they feel is right, means they are disliked then that is fine, they are willing to be disliked and unpopular, in the long term their integrity and congruence shines through. Effective leadership is not about being a *'goody-goody two shoes'* and trying to keep everyone happy, but making the right decision at the right time, even if not an overly favourable step.

The great Indian spiritual master and Guru, Yogiji Maharaj often used to teach profound wisdom through simple tales and analogies. He used to often narrate the story of the farmer and his wife who made their way into town on a bull. They started their journey with the farmer sitting on the back of the bull and his wife walking on foot. Seeing this, people criticised the farmer - how can a man sit comfortably whilst making a woman walk! Hearing this, they changed places and now the wife sat on the bull, only to be criticised by the people once again - how can a woman sit comfortably and make her poor husband walk! Hearing this they both decided to sit on the bull but were criticised by the people once again - oh dear look at these two cruel individuals, they will break that poor bull's back! Finally, they felt they had the solution to avoid any more criticism, they both decided to walk either side of the bull and let the bull walk in the middle, only to find that the people now laughed and said - look at these two-silly people, they have a bull but they are not using it! The moral of this story for leaders is that it is impossible to please all of the people all of the time. As a leader you need to develop the strength of character to stick to your convictions.

The Greek Philosopher Aristotle has famously said:

"Know thyself. . ."

As a leader you have to know yourself and know which direction you are heading, after all you are the captain of the ship. The people in your team and in your family, are relying on you to be at your best and provide vision, energy, motivation and direction. All of this can be a tall order and very demanding on your inner resources which is why it is imperative that you regularly take the time to maintain your health and wellbeing. As a leader you have a duty to yourself and those around you to do basic things, such as eat healthy and exercise regularly, but it is also important for you to take rest and recharge your battery in whatever way works for you: go and meditate in your cave, take a walk with nature, or punch a boxing bag. Go and do whatever you need to do to re-energise yourself and be at your best, you owe it to yourself and your team.

Constant Growth and Learning

Have you ever observed a baby's eyes? They are filled with curiosity and wonderment at everything around them and if you observe them carefully enough, you can almost see when they are making connections and making sense of the world around them. As children we were fascinated by the world and we had questions we were desperate to find the answers to, we were constantly learning and growing. The leader that is dedicated to their own personal development and self-mastery must be a learner, they must be open to new ideas and new experiences and approach the world with that same sense of wonderment and curiosity that they had as a child.

Many leaders stop learning because they feel they know everything there is to know, this is a dangerous viewpoint for any leader. Life is full of change and what you may know today can be completely irrelevant tomorrow, a leader that does not learn can be left behind by the speed of change and their leadership can become ineffective and out of date. The Stanford University Psychology Professor, Carol Dweck, defines two types of mindsets or paradigms: one is a person who has a fixed mindset and the other is a person that has a growth mindset. People with a fixed mindset believe that their level of skill, knowledge or ability is fixed, that they are either good at maths or not good, they are creative or not very creative, they have a fixed viewpoint and that's the end of the story. However, people who hold a growth mindset believe that their level of skill, knowledge or ability can develop and can improve. A person with a growth mindset might not be good at maths but believes that with effort and training they can get better. If you are to develop great leadership ability then you must develop a growth mindset, which means you hold the belief that you can improve many aspects of your life and your ability through training and your personal efforts.

These days, the solutions to many of your problems are literally sitting in your pocket. With so many people having access to the internet, it means that we are able to access and share more knowledge and information faster than at any other time in human history! We are experiencing an information explosion like never before and the phone sitting in your pocket is capable of finding the answer to a mind-boggling number of questions you may have, just Google it! Leaders are readers and books are the training weights of the mind, the more you read and learn, the better you will be as an individual and as a leader. Develop the habit of reading and learning - it will serve you well along your leadership journey, providing you with perspective, insight and a depth of understanding.

A young man once went to a Zen Master eager to learn from the Master. He started speaking about his understanding of the practice of Zen whilst the Master poured the young man a cup of tea. The young man carried on speaking and the Master carried on pouring the tea until the teacup began to overflow, the young man shouted stop! The Master then explained that just like the overflowing cup, he was full of preconceived ideas but for him to learn from the Master, he must first empty the cup so that he can taste the Master's cup of tea. Leaders need mentors and coaches and they need to surround themselves with people that are operating at a higher level than them. Surrounding yourself with people that are more successful than you, allows you to raise your standards to higher levels - as a leader you should develop the humility of a dedicated student, open to learning and experience. Always be vigilant in that you do not become too egotistical that you stop learning!

You vs. You

In some countries, access to trucks or construction vehicles is limited and so, to carry heavy loads on building sites elephants are used. There is a way in which the elephant is trained for this job. When the elephant is a baby, one of its feet is tied to a small wooden stump in the ground and the baby elephant tries desperately to get away, it struggles and tries but fails to get away because it is only small in size. As that elephant grows and becomes a full sized large elephant, that is powerful enough to uproot a tree, the amazing thing is that the trainer can tie the fully-grown elephant to the same small wooden stump which the trainer used when it was a baby and the elephant does not move. It stands still and does not even try to get away. The elephant believes in its mind that it is impossible to get away from the small wooden stump in the ground, after all it had tried and failed as a baby so it does not bother to even try despite having grown even stronger! We may also have limiting beliefs in our mind that hold us back from fulfilling our true potential as leaders, far worse than someone else putting us down is when we put ourselves down and do not believe in ourselves.

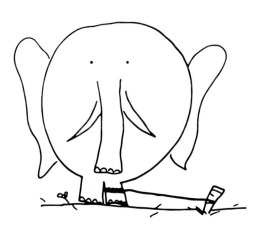

Self-mastery develops self-belief, we believe in ourselves, our vision and the direction we are going. We have faith that everything in the end will work out, this belief is the starting point of great leadership. After all, how can you expect others to believe in you as a leader when you do not even believe in yourself? Changing our thinking patterns, changing the words we speak and changing our habits and behaviours is going to be an uphill struggle at times and it will feel like a real battle, the battleground is your own mind. You have a negative voice and a positive voice within your own mind, they are like two armies constantly at war and for most people the army of the negative voice wins most of the time, it's just you vs. you and the path of self-mastery is about training yourself so that your positive voice wins and shines through.

Leadership is about bringing the best of yourself to inspire, engage and motivate other people. When your thoughts, emotions, words, and actions are under your control you can, as a leader, make the right moves, you can think before you move, just like in a game of chess. Aristotle once said:

'Anybody can become angry - that is easy, but to be angry with the right person and to the right degree and at the right time and for the right purpose and in the right way - that is not within everybody's power and is not easy.'

Your self-mastery will allow you to develop this skill so that as a leader you can express anger, annoyance or disappointment, but you do so in a skilful way as a tool to push the people you lead to higher levels of personal growth and output. Often leaders that do not have a handle over their own emotions and habits, create havoc for their teams and families, they are unable to lead others because they cannot lead themselves. Master your thoughts, master your emotions, master your words, master your habits and you will be a great leader.

In the Hollywood movie, *'The Shawshank Redemption'*, an innocent man accused of murdering his wife makes a daring escape from prison by crawling through miles of piping filled with raw sewage. A disgusting and stomach churning prospect to even think about. In the end, he is a free man and lives the rest of his life near a beautiful beach. To be motivated and determined enough to crawl through miles of sewage, you have to be in a pretty bad situation. Real and lasting change often comes about in our life when we have really hit rock bottom. When you are so extremely frustrated and angry at the state of affairs, your life and yourself, this can be the catalyst for great change. The great thing about hitting rock bottom is that the only way is up! I am regularly involved with coaching leaders and people from all walks of life helping them to commit to making positive changes in their life. The question I always ask is, do you really want it? Do you really want to change? Changing yourself can be tough and uncomfortable but the crazy fact is that progress only happens in the uncomfortable zone. If you find your gym workout or exercise routine comfortable you are probably not getting much benefit from it, this applies to everything. Leaders are willing to work on themselves and be uncomfortable because they know that is where progress lies. You may not have to climb through miles of sewage to get to your beach but you will have to be motivated enough to go through discomfort and pain to really make positive and lasting changes in your life, it will be tough but it will definitely be worth it.

Summary Key Points & Self Reflection

1. What negative thoughts and words regularly occur that

   stop you from reaching your potential?

   _____

   _____

   _____

   _____

2. Write down positive thoughts and words that you can use

   to challenge your own negativity.

   _____

   _____

   _____

   _____

3. Describe what actions you are going to take when faced with a challenge?

_____

_____

_____

_____

4. What practical actions can you implement to ensure you are at your best every day?

_____

_____

_____

_____

5. Write down how you think you will feel when you have transformed your negative thoughts, words actions to more positive thoughts, words and actions?

_____

_____

_____

_____

Notes

Chapter 4

THE POWER OF CERTAINTY

If you consider some of the world's best known and most trusted brands such as Nike, Apple, and Coca-Cola, they all promise to deliver an amazing experience to the customer. The advertising and marketing behind the world's best brands deliver messages with certainty, promises are packaged as guarantees. Nike believes it is the world's best trainer, it's advertising reflects its confidence in this belief, just as Apple exudes absolute certainty about the supremacy of its position as the world's best personal computer. Consumers buy into confidence, they buy into certainty. Leaders, like brands, need to be definitive, certainty and confidence makes people feel safe and secure. The certainty of the leader makes others feel like they can trust them and that they are in safe hands.

The surgeon tells you he is one of the best in the world at performing the heart transplant procedure, you see all his qualifications and certificates hanging on the wall of his office. He talks you through the procedure with absolute clarity and confidence, he reassures you that he has performed ninety-nine heart transplant operations before and that you are his 100th patient and you will be fine. As he is wheeling you into theatre, a question occurs in your mind and so you ask, *'Doctor how many of the ninety-nine operations were successful?'*, He answers, *'None, but I am feeling very confident about you, don't worry!'*.

Leaders may project confidence or certainty but if it is not backed up by competence, it will not create trust and dedication from people. Competence always has to come before confidence, not the other way around. Developing your competence as a leader comes through experience, you will go through challenging times and every obstacle you overcome will build your confidence and your sense of certainty.

The personal disciplines and the path of self-mastery that we examined in the last chapter, allows a leader to be certain at a deeper level of their being, so even when everything is unstable and troublesome there is self-confidence that shines through the darkness. The leader is like the lighthouse in a storm, guiding the people to safety. We live in a world full of insecurity, change and uncertainty and when a leader comes along that has built up their competence and as a result has a sense of certainty about how to navigate difficult times, they provide the people they lead with one of the most important and basic of human needs, security.

What is it that makes a leader, a leader? What is the core element of leadership? Knowing. Knowing who we are and knowing where we are going. The leader knows - they set the direction. Leadership and management are two different things, organizations and businesses need both managers and leaders, both functions are valuable but there are key differences between them. Leading people successfully through times of change, difficulty and uncertainty requires leadership, not just management. Leadership is about articulating a compelling vision for the future and aligning people towards that vision. It is your job as a leader to keep people moving and motivated in the right direction and guiding them through the uncertainty.

Change is Inevitable

Harnessing the power of certainty and leading people through change, begins with accepting the fact that change is inevitable. You look out of your bedroom window on a cold winter morning, a beautiful untouched pure white sheet of snow shines back at you, you decide to build a snowman. Great conditions and plenty of snow, you set about building your masterpiece. Your glistening creation stands tall and stout and proud of your achievement you find yourself shouting out, '*my snowman will NEVER melt!*' The neighbours decide you have finally lost the plot. The next morning, the sun comes out and within a short space of time, a hat, a carrot and a scarf is all that remains of your snowman – snowmen melt. Change, just like death and taxes, is of course inevitable. As a leader, it is wise for you to cooperate with the inevitable.

Today, organizations, businesses, teams and individuals face an unprecedented pace of change. The lightning speed of technological advances, a highly competitive global marketplace, an ever-changing economy and changing values and social norms, means that change is simply a fact of life. Change features in so many aspects of our society and is part and parcel of nature. Think of the seasons, the weather and the planets; even our bodies - red blood cells change every four months. As leaders we have to accept change and not resist against the changes that we will face. Leaders have two challenges when it comes to change, firstly, how can they individually deal with the change and secondly, how will they successfully help others through the change. The power of certainty is the ability to mentally deal with change and crisis, to be certain in your own abilities, and to provide certainty to those that you lead.

As a leader, you have to change with change and there is a great danger in not doing so. One of the most powerful secrets of success for individuals, businesses and organizations in our modern world is developing the ability to be flexible, agile and open to change. When the old ways of doing things are no longer suitable to meet new challenges and when the rules of the game change, organizations and individuals have to be able to move with the change. Just as in nature, there is the law of evolution and as a leader, for you and your people, the danger of not evolving is extinction. If you want to truly develop into a powerful leader, you must approach leadership with a mindset that accepts and embraces change.

The weather forecast predicts an upcoming snow storm, you realise you do not want a snowman, you need an igloo! You do not wait for the sun to melt your snowman; you proactively break your snowman first and initiate the change process to create an igloo. When something's not working great leaders initiate change. To initiate any successful change process, whether in large corporate organizations, businesses, educational institutions, or families, leaders have to first fully and clearly understand the reason why the change must take place, why the current way of doing things must change and to communicate this reason constantly, gain interest and involve the people in the change process. Communication and involvement are key ingredients in getting people to move in the direction you want them to go in. Leaders provide certainty that the change is needed and they provide certainty about the way forward.

Leaders Emerge in Crisis

Conscious leaders implement change when it's time to change, but sometimes change is thrust upon leaders. Unexpected and unwanted change really tests your ability as a leader. In fact, it could be argued that your true leadership abilities will only ever be proven when facing crisis. Just as priceless diamonds are formed only under immense pressure, a leader only proves themselves at times of crisis. A situation where everything is going wrong, where drastic change has happened and people are feeling a massive sense of uncertainty, they look to the leader to be the rock, to provide stability and support. In a crisis, leaders need mental resiliency and hardiness to help others navigate through crisis.

Soldiers train for war, they train to be able to survive in highly stressful, extreme environments. The training and recruitment of some of the world's most elite armed forces, such as the US Navy Seals or the SAS, have rigorous training programmes that new recruits are put through. They are tested to the limits of their physical, mental and emotional capacities and many will not complete their training, the drop-out rate is high, only the most determined make it successfully to the end of their training as a fully qualified Navy Seal or SAS Soldier. The training of these elite soldiers focuses to a large extent on developing the right mindset, training the mind becomes even more important than training the physical body. When crisis strikes, it is the leader who has to have control over their own thoughts and reactions. Leaders should be prepared for chaos, emergencies and the unexpected crisis.

As a leader you need to develop a state of alertness, a readiness for battle. You need to develop a state of mind that allows you to cope with pressure and strain, to be able to deal effectively with all the small and large fires that will come your way without being overly flustered. Many leaders want to make their life easy, they have a natural tendency to procrastinate, to not face up to burning issues and like the ostrich, bury their heads in the sand. How do such leaders react when an inevitable crisis hits? They panic just like everyone else, their decisions are dictated by their emotions and they become poor leaders of their organizations, businesses or families. True leaders train for crisis like soldiers' train for war, they dedicate themselves to mastering their thoughts, words and habits so that they can be certain in uncertainty and show leadership at times of crisis. As a leader you need to train yourself to develop mental resiliency and hardiness by putting yourself through personal and professional challenges, not avoiding issues like the ostrich.

During the 9/11 attacks on the twin towers in New York, the firefighters were involved in risking their own lives to enter the towers and rescue people. This involved entering the towers that were on fire and very unstable, to look for survivors and people that were trapped. The remains of the towers could collapse further at any moment but they showed great courage and a sense of certainty in uncertainty, they showed leadership. These firefighters may have felt great fear, uncertainty and doubt within themselves, but they were able to put that to one side and focus on the job of leading others to safety, they did not think of their own safety. It is common to see in the corporate world and in many businesses, leaders who put their own selfish needs above the needs of the people they lead. They seek to protect themselves and line their own pockets first. Leaders that implement job cuts as their first and only solution to financial challenges, create further uncertainty for people in a crisis. The primary aim of the leader who uses the power of certainty is to make their people feel safe and secure when facing change or a crisis.

Reactions to Change

People react to change or a crisis situation in many different ways. It is important for the leader to respond effectively to all the different emotional reactions that they may face from the team. One man who is stuck in traffic complains and moans, whilst another uses the time to listen to the radio and enjoy the view, both are delayed but what a difference in their experience of this event. The same boiling water that softens a potato, hardens an egg. In life we often see two people who may experience the same life event but have totally different reactions to it. No matter how well a leader may know their people and the individual strengths and weaknesses of each team member, it is difficult to predict with 100% accuracy how people are going to react. A leader can at best anticipate reactions and know how to deal with different reactions as they come up.

A typical reaction to change is feeling helpless, feeling overwhelmed and out of control. These people are really struggling to cope with the change, they have very negative feelings towards it and feel like they are victims. Another common reaction is anger, annoyance and criticism, people who are critics can be of two kinds: those that just simply criticise the change with no other value to add to the situation and critics who, although they may sound very negative, actually have something valuable to say, their criticism is constructive in some way. Victims needs reassurance that everything will be fine, critics may need to be given the space to vent their frustration and feel they have been listened to. However, it is important that the leader tries to makes sure that critics do not express their feelings too openly in front of other team members as negative emotions can spread like wild fire. The leader should also listen carefully to a critical team member, there may be something of real value within the criticism that could be useful or should be implemented. Leaders should not just simply ignore the critic, they should seek to listen to and address their concerns.

Another reaction that a team member may have is no reaction! You cannot really tell what they are thinking or what they are feeling, they seem to be totally neutral. Certain people do not seem to express much emotion when change or a crisis takes place, there could be various reasons for this. It could be that they are indifferent to the change. They are not bothered by it and have no feelings about it either way. It could be that they do have feelings about the change but are keeping it to themselves, this could be dangerous for you as a leader. At least with the victim and the critic you know where you stand in terms of how they really feel, the neutral reaction of a bystander may need you to do some one-to-one coaching to really ascertain how they feel. Sitting on the fence and not wanting to rock the boat or upset people, could be a reason for the bystander's neutral reaction, but it is important for you as a leader to understand their true thoughts and feelings, as not knowing could cause you and the team problems further down the road. Our true feelings have a funny way of showing up in our thoughts, words and actions.

You could of course have team members that take the change all in their stride, these are the navigators of the team that can navigate the change with reasonable ease and comfort, they may even feel excited by the change. A strategic leader can use these people to have a positive impact on other team members who may be dragging their heels, for example teaming up a victim with a navigator could help the victim see the change in a different light and help them through. The navigator may even be a positive influence on a critic, but it is the leader's job to manage all the different reactions and emotions that their people may experience as a result of the change. Giving each individual what they require is a skill that great leaders acquire through experience, they are able to give their team members a sense of certainty, that despite the changes, everything is going to be okay.

VICTIM   CRITIC

BYSTANDER   NAVIGATOR

Certainty in Uncertainty

Great leaders have the ability to be certain in uncertainty, they are able to keep their cool and think clearly amidst chaos and change. A leader keeps their head stable when everyone else around them is losing control. The ability to think clearly and make the right decision is crucial. In order for the leader to successfully navigate change and lead their team forwards, they must have a clear idea of what they can control, and maintain some influence over those things they have absolutely no control over. Knowing what you control and what you do not control as a leader is key, not feeling overwhelmed but making good decisions. This idea about how we think about what we can and cannot control, has been expressed beautifully in the Serenity Prayer:

'God, grant me the SERENITY to ACCEPT the things I cannot change, the COURAGE to CHANGE the things I can and the WISDOM to know the DIFFERENCE'

There is a logic and rationality behind these words that simply makes sense. There are certain things that will happen to you or your team, that you as leader will be unable to change, there is nothing you can do about these things. These are all matters that are outside your sphere of control as a leader. If you cannot change a situation, if you are unable to undo what has been done, if you are powerless to influence a certain situation then it makes clear and rational sense not to worry and not to become stressed. This is sometimes difficult to do because we are creatures of emotion, but if we can learn to train our minds to think clearly it can help us to deal with the things we cannot control with more composure, as the old proverb says, *'it's no use crying over spilt milk'*, it's already spilt and crying is not going to help the situation. As a leader, if you can learn to accept certain situations with as much serenity as you can muster, then it will help you to make better decisions. In the case of spilt milk, getting a mop might be a good starting point!

Once you have fully accepted that there are certain things outside your control, the next question to ask yourself as a leader is, what can I do? What can I change? What can I influence? What is in my sphere of control? Great leaders are solution focused rather than problem focused, that is to say they focus on finding solutions or moving forwards in some way, rather than being stuck with the problem. Human beings have an amazing ability to interpret events and give meaning to the things that happen to us. This ability can be very empowering for you as a leader if you choose to interpret events in a positive way, even the worst of disasters may have some seed of good or some lesson that can be learnt. Training yourself as a leader to look for the good, look for a solution, brings control back to you. Leaders are courageous and at times of change or crisis courage is needed, the courage to move forwards and the courage to change the things that you can change, for example you may not have a time machine that would allow you to change the past, but you can choose a positive way to interpret the past so you and your team can now start to look towards the future.

A big part of being certain at times of uncertainty, comes down to the leader's ability to think clearly about what they can and cannot control. This ability to know the difference will help the leader make better decisions, stay calm under pressure and use their time effectively to lead their team through the change. Whether or not you have control or influence over a situation may not be a clear-cut answer. Sometimes, you may feel there are certain situations you have a degree of influence over; sometimes you may feel very strongly about being able to change and control a situation which everybody else around you feel is unchangeable. You, as the leader, have to make that call and take action to do what you can and you must try your best not to unnecessarily spend your time and energy worrying about things outside your control. This is what it means to be a wise and strategic leader.

Know the Direction

Leaders trying to implement or respond to change have to lead and guide people through the change. A captain of a ship has to be aware of many things. They should know their crew members, they should know the weather conditions and the potential dangers they may face at sea, but above all else they should know where they are going. They should know the direction. As a leader, you are the captain of your ship. It is your job to set the direction of your organization, set the direction of your business, set the direction of your family. Thereafter, the often-forgotten step is to communicate that direction to your team. When you know where you are going as a leader you have a sense of certainty, when your people know where they are going they feel safe and secure. The leader's certainty of direction gives the team certainty of direction, the ship can move forward.

The art and science of leading change is being able to align your team with your direction, your vision and your strategy. You will face resistance and as a leader you have to understand the reasons why individuals may resist change. Individuals have personalities and so do organizations. The personality of an organization or even a family unit, is often referred to as the culture. As a leader trying to change things, you must take into account the positive and negative aspects of your organization's culture. Families, businesses and teams may have set ways of doing things, cultural norms that could be very anti-productive, negative or even destructive. Leaders that fail to understand not only the individuals in their team but also the wider culture in which they operate, can fail to align people with a new way of doing things, often resulting in low morale and tensions.

So many leaders fear making decisions as they do not want to risk being disliked as a result. Effective leaders are willing to be disliked and make unpopular decisions if needed. It is impossible for a leader to please everyone at all times and decisions have to be made. People are less upset or disengaged when they clearly understand the rationale and reasoning behind a leader's decision, they still may not agree but at least the leader has attempted to explain their thinking. As a leader, you need to constantly communicate your reasons for the decisions you make and the direction you have set. If you do not have a plan for your life, your business or your family then someone else does. Today, we are bombarded by the media trying to sell us the perfect life, competitors are trying to steal your people and exploit your weaknesses. For example, if you do not have a set of values and guidelines you would like your children to follow in life, then the influence of television shows, films and the internet will provide plenty of ways to keep the ideas flowing, but not necessarily the right ones! As a leader, know your direction with certainty, have a plan, have a vision and set the direction.

How do you motivate people? How do you get people to move in the direction you want them to go? People move and are willing to change when there are personal consequences for not changing. The threat of job loss, for example, might be a strong motivator for change, this is the '*stick*' approach to leadership and it does have its uses. The '*carrot*' approach to moving people is to offer rewards and benefits, such as a pay rise or medical insurance and again this could be a useful motivator in certain circumstances. However, what can motivate people beyond sticks and carrots is a good leader that really understands people and is able to provide a sense of purpose and value in their work. People are moved by a compelling vision and by their feelings about their work and great leaders know how to ignite the passion of the individuals within their team to follow the direction set by them.

Leading Through Change

Being a good leader is a lot like being a good parent. For those of you that are parents to young children, you almost expect that your children are not going to do everything you say the first time you ask them to do it. If you have teenagers then you may possibly have a great deal of seasoned experience with people not listening to you and giving you plenty of resistance! Good parents do not give up on their children. They stick with them through all the trials and tribulations of growing up and beyond. Good parents listen, they are firm when they need to be firm and gentle when they need to be gentle, but above everything else they are patient.

Implementing organizational and business change also requires patience. A good leader is patient with the members of their team. Change will not happen overnight, mistakes will be made but that should not mean that a leader should resort to firing people as the first port of call. Great leaders have the spirit of working with people and developing them.

You may be certain about your direction and the vision for the future but to reach your destination you need the dedication and commitment of your people. If your team have not bought in to your vision then it is like trying to fly a kite indoors, it will not get off the ground! You need to rally your team around your vision, get the support you need so people want to grab their desk fans and open the windows to get that kite lifted in the air.

Keep the following points in mind when trying to get that commitment from your people:

- Create an environment of trust and openness;
- Pitch your message effectively and understand your audience;
- Be clear and transparent in your communication;
- Remember everyone's favourite radio station – WIFM! (What's in It for Me!).

Change begins at the top. As a leader you have to exemplify the changes you want to make. You have to become a role model and a champion of the new culture, or the new way of working which you are trying to implement amongst your team and wider organization. You may know your goal and you may know your strategy but you are not above the rules. Whenever leaders make statements about desired results and people do not see these behaviours being modelled by the leaders themselves, it can create a sense of mistrust and cynicism towards the new change. As a leader you need to harness the power of certainty by walking your talk.

The hardest part of a rocket's journey into space is leaving the earth's orbit because it has to move against the gravitational pull of the earth. Similarly, implementing change as a leader is tough, you will need great strength, energy, enthusiasm and hard work to really implement and embed change. Do not give up on your efforts, expect resistors, understand them, communicate them to your people but most of all, being patient and persevering is key. As a leader you will create certainty about the vision you are trying to implement if you commit yourself and engage others in the process. Make sure you do not forget to celebrate small wins and successes as you go through change. With a sense of humour, strong communication skills and an appreciation for everyone's efforts, these traits will serve you well as you navigate and implement change. Always remember, leaders need to be certain to make others feel certain.

Summary Key Points & Self Reflection

1. What changes have you handled well or felt excited about? Why were these changes easy to deal with?

    _____

    _____

    _____

    _____

2. What changes have you been very critical of and why? Were there more constructive, positive, creative solutions or approaches you could have applied?

    _____

    _____

    _____

    _____

3. In your organization or team, how would you show, articulate and communicate to others that change is needed and necessary?

_____

_____

_____

_____

4. List some of the cultural barriers that would make the change difficult to implement in your team or organization, as well as some solutions to overcome those barriers.

_____

_____

_____

_____

5. Think of examples from your personal or professional life where the consequences of not changing have been the primary motivation for the change?

    _____

    _____

    _____

    _____

6. Who do you think should be involved in the change process and how will you ensure they are involved?

    _____

    _____

    _____

    _____

Notes

Chapter 5

THE POWER OF TRUST

Your leadership adventure will take on a new meaning when you harness the immense power of trust, the last of the powerful leadership secrets we will explore in this book. The power of trust works in many ways. It begins with the principle of self-trust, developing trust and confidence in our own ability as leaders. When we trust ourselves, we are more likely to gain the trust of others; gaining the trust of others also involves becoming congruent so that our thoughts, words and actions match up. We keep the promises to ourselves so our self-esteem and self-worth can grow every day, as a result we like ourselves and trust ourselves. We keep the promises to the people around us so that other people trust us and know that we deliver on what we say. Harnessing the power of trust as a leader also involves trusting others. Truly great leaders put trust and faith into the people around them. They are patient with them and they allow others to grow into leaders themselves.

The Chinese bamboo tree is an interesting plant, it requires water, soil and sunshine like most plants. However even after a year of providing all of these elements you cannot see any visible signs of growth above the surface. In the second year you carry on providing regular water and everything that the plant might need to grow, but sill you see no growth above the soil. Now, just think about it, if you tended regularly to a seed for two years and saw nothing grow above the soil, you would give up, am I right? Let's say you don't give up and you carry on watering the non-visible plant for a third year and a fourth, but still nothing appears, no visible signs of growth. However, in the fifth year something extraordinary happens, the Chinese bamboo tree grows eighty feet tall in just six weeks!

Now here is the key question, did the Chinese bamboo tree really grow eighty feet in six weeks? Was it the case that this plant did nothing for four years, remained completely dormant and then suddenly decided to grow like crazy in the fifth year? Actually, the exponential growth of the plant in the fifth year is because of what was happening underground during the first four years. This little tree was busy growing underground, developing the strong roots and foundations that would be able to support its massive growth spurt above the surface in the fifth year and beyond. The strong roots underground was crucial to develop because they would provide the foundational support that the tree needs to reach its full potential growth. The same principle is true for leaders building trust within their organizations.

Trust does not develop instantly. It takes time and effort to build the foundations of a trusting relationship. Leaders have to be able to develop trust in their people and people have to be able to develop trust in their leaders, it's a two-way thing. Both parties in a relationship have to work at delivering on promises and being congruent but it begins with the leader. The leader needs the faith and the patient perseverance to keep toiling away at the vision they have for the organization, business or family. There may be times when a leader sees no tangible evidence of progress, this can be very frustrating for leaders who commonly feel that things are not progressing as fast as they should do. At times like this the leader can spend time nurturing relationships, listening to people, addressing concerns and really understanding their individuals, thereby laying the foundations for growth, change and massive future success. Nurturing the roots as a leader is about creating a loyal and committed team that believe in what you, as a leader, are trying to achieve. This will take time and sacrifice on your part, there are no short cuts to building trust, but it will be worth it.

Think Win/Win and Beyond!

One of the major reasons for employee dissatisfaction in the workplace is a bad relationship with one's supervisor or manager. The worst type of leaders are the ones who exploit and take advantage of their people, for example a leader may overwork and underpay their employees. The leader only thinks of themselves and believes in themselves winning and their employees losing. The win/lose style of leadership is bad for business. Ultimately these types of leaders and the organizations they run cannot deliver optimal results. Disengaged or fearful employees are not going to be motivated to put 100% effort into their work, why should they? Deep down their feelings of injustice about their job and feelings of resentment towards their manager will mean they may do what is required to keep their jobs, but would jump ship in a flash should another job present itself.

Good leaders think in terms of win/win. They understand clearly that their success depends on their team and the individuals that comprise of that team. It has often been stated that an organization's most important asset is its people, so leaders that can offer their employees a mutually beneficial relationship will get better motivation and productivity out of their people. Mutually beneficial symbiotic relationships are found everywhere in nature, for example, in Africa an Oxpecker bird sits on the back of a Zebra and eats the ticks, the Zebra is providing the food for the Oxpecker and the bird is providing a pest control service for the Zebra, by getting rid of the ticks that are causing it a nuisance. The relationship works because both parties benefit from each other, much like a boss providing a job with career prospects and good money, and the employee giving their time and efforts, working hard to further the cause of the organization or business.

Great leaders think beyond just win/win. The '*I scratch your back and you scratch mine*' way of looking at the world is transactional, it is the way the world works. We have all heard the saying that money makes the world go around. However, people can be motivated and inspired by more than just financial rewards and they often do things because it feels good and because it is the right thing to do. Some of the greatest leaders in the world are the ones that give without expectation of return. They are the ones that give of themselves, their time and their energy because it is the right thing to do, not because they want something in return. Beyond win/win means that a leader gives, that they create meaning, purpose and joy for those who they lead. This type of leadership comes from a genuine place of wanting to help and develop others. Leaders that operate beyond win/win create teams and organizational cultures that are willing to go the extra mile because they want to, because they love what they do, because they believe fully in the vision, not because it is expected or for something in return.

India is the largest democracy in the world and one of the most universally loved and respected presidents of the nation was APJ Abdul Kalam. He had a very down to earth and simple demeanor and despite his extensive intellectual gifts he was a leader that was able to connect with the people. President Abdul Kalam would ask himself a very simple but powerful question whenever he met with anyone, whether it be a child, an elderly person, rich or poor and the question was, 'what can I give?' Most people and many leaders spend their lives asking, 'what can I take?' Imagine if you started to ask yourself what can I give to my employees? My team members? My family members and anyone else that you meet in your life? Giving does not mean money or gifts it means simple things like a smile, your time, acknowledgment, a listening ear. Sometimes simple ideas are the really powerful ones and asking this simple question can transform your leadership and the personal satisfaction you experience in life.

Building Trust Through Congruence

Do we trust our politicians? Do we trust the news stories reported in the media? Do we trust the door to door salesman? Do we trust our neighbours or even our family members? We live in a world where technology, with its ease and speed of communication, means our lives are becoming ever more transparent and the inconsistencies in people's behaviour are highlighted and communicated much more widely than in the past. It has become increasingly difficult for leaders to hide a shadowy past or keep mistakes a secret. We come across incongruence all the time, leaders that promise one thing but do not deliver on their promises. Leaders that are incongruent, whose words and actions do not match up, can create feelings of mistrust amongst the people they lead. If people do not believe in what you say, your words loose power and significance. If people do not believe you will deliver on your promises then your influence as a leader is greatly undermined.

The secret to building trust is your commitment as a leader to deliver on your promises and do what you say, do what you are going to do. It is always better for you as a leader to under promise and over deliver. The last thing you want to be known as is as a person who speaks big words and says all the right things but when it comes to the crunch, fail to live up to your words. You have to be very conscious in your communications with your team and the people you lead - that you sincerely mean every word that you speak. It would be far better for you as a leader to speak less words but ensure the words you do speak manifest themselves into tangible results. Actions always speak louder than words and it is what you actually do as a leader that counts, not what you say you are going to do.

We are being watched all the time, after all you are the leader. What you say, what you do, your personality and your character traits all get observed and talked about amongst the people you lead. Some issues people will tell you directly, some issues you may overhear people talking about which could involve discussions regarding your leadership and you as a person, which may well happen behind your back. All this comes with the package of being a leader, if you cannot handle the reality of people gossiping about you and have a hard time with people making judgements about your character, then leadership is not for you. It is impossible for a leader to keep everyone happy all of the time and there will always be people who see the worst in us or highlight our faults to others. However, we have a duty to ourselves and our businesses, organizations and families to be as consistent and as congruent a leader as possible. Our thoughts, our words and our actions have to be matched up, this is how we strive to get people to trust us.

Leaders are human, they make mistakes, they have faults, weaknesses and failings. Your people do not expect you to be superhuman, they do not expect perfection but they do expect you to be honest. People do not like being lied to, they also dislike pretence or fake behaviour, most people can see through someone who is pretending to be something they are not. Be real, be genuine and be honest, it is amazing to see just how many leaders have a real problem owning up to their mistakes or admitting when something has gone wrong. Leaders who try to cover up their mistakes or faults with lies and excuses can really disengage their people, it can create a massive sense of mistrust. Your people just need to know that you are doing your best, that you are genuinely striving to be a congruent person, if you're honest when you have slipped up, then you are more likely to gain the respect and trust of your people.

True Delegation

As a leader you are not going to be able to do everything, nor do you have the required skillset, experience and knowledge to do everything. Every successful leader who has taken their business or organization to great heights has not done so alone, they have built a team who have been behind the leader and supported their vision. Successful leaders understand very clearly their own strengths and weaknesses and they understand very clearly the individual strengths and weaknesses of the individuals in their team. Two of the most important assets you possess as a leader are your time and your energy. The majority of, and ideally, all of your time and energy, should be spent working on your strengths, the tasks that only you can do as the leader. Setting the vision and strategy, growing the business, developing new ideas, building relationships with external and internal stakeholders, keeping everyone excited and passionate about what they are doing - these are some of the bigger elements that leaders should be spending their time and energy on.

How can leaders spend all, or the majority of their time, working on their core strengths? They need to delegate everything else. Delegation is about trust, trusting your team that they can and will deliver. Many leaders have a hard time delegating effectively. There are leaders that do not trust anyone else to do certain jobs that should be delegated so the leader ends up doing these jobs themselves, which means the leader is not using their time or energy effectively, in fact they are wasting the most precious assets they have as leaders. The other type of leader is the one who delegates but does not provide enough information, or delegates the wrong task to the wrong person. The leader may get upset when they discover the job has not been carried out to their satisfaction but the fault lies with the leader. Delegation is not just a matter of putting high workloads onto other people, it is about intelligently selecting people to carry out work, clearly setting the context and giving them all the information and support they may need.

It is the leader's duty to make sure that the person to whom they have delegated a task to is happy and comfortable with that task. To delegate a task to someone who feels overwhelmed by the task, or feels it is beyond their capacity to deliver, can erode the trust between the leader and the team member. There is an art to delegating effectively, it does require some thought on the part of the leader and is not just a case of letting people get on with it. Leaders have to follow up, provide guidance and keep people on track and at the same time be very mindful of micro-managing. The idea is that leaders should overlook but not micro-manage. When people feel they are being micro-managed they switch off and become very disengaged which hinders trust. Effective delegation is a balancing act, it is the art of trusting your people by selecting the right person for the right job, providing them with everything they need to do the job and then allowing them the freedom to deliver, but still providing guidance as and when needed.

What is your reaction if you delegate something to someone and they do not do a good job, or it all goes horribly wrong - it turns out to be a disaster? Many leaders in this situation look to blame their people, they may even get extremely upset and discipline their employees; these types of reactions from the leader can do a lot of damage to the relationship between the leader and the people that they lead. Trust is such a powerful asset and leaders that point fingers and do not allow for mistakes, destroy this powerful and valuable asset. When you delegate something to your people, trust them. When you delegate something to your people and it does not turn out right, allow for mistakes, coach them and move on, this will build trust in your leadership.

It's Not About You

'I intend to be a servant not a leader; as one above others. I pledge to use all my strength and ability to live up to the world's expectations of me'

Nelson Mandela

What exactly does it mean to be a leader? Volumes and volumes of books have been written trying to answer this question. Leadership is such a fascinating area of research because it covers all areas of human endeavour, from family life to politics, to battle zones to the classroom, the boardroom and beyond; you name it, anywhere groups of people come together for a specific purpose, they require a leader. One of the biggest misconceptions and sadly a very common one, is that a leader can hold inside their minds the thought that being a leader is only about the exercise of power over others. To believe that because you are a leader you are now somehow above other people and you have the right to exercise control over them, is very erroneous.

Human history has been filled with despots and tyrants whose megalomania has known no bounds. Their massive egos have led to the ruin of nations and even today we are faced with leaders in all walks of life who believe it is all about them! They lead from their ego. These types of leaders make decisions with their ego at the centre point, their decisions are biased, selfish, narrow-minded and filled with their own agendas, this can be terrible for team morale and disastrous for business. Truly great leaders see leadership in a very different light, they understand that being a leader is not about them at all. It is all about serving others. The greatest and most powerful definition of leadership is that a leader is a servant, their duty above everything else is to serve.

If you approached your position as the leader of your business, the leader of your organization or the leader of your family as a servant, just think about how different your mindset would be as opposed to approaching your leadership position with the mindset of, *'I am in control!'* A servant's primary duty is to serve, a servant would listen, a servant would not have an ego about getting stuck in and doing what needs to be done. The greatest leaders are humble and humility is one of the most powerful

141

leadership secrets you can ever strive to imbibe in your life. If you are in a position of power and you only exercise that power for the greater good, to serve others and you do so with humility, then you gain a massive amount of respect, admiration and most importantly, trust from the people you lead.

Being humble as a leader can come in many forms and it is a difficult trait to imbibe within us but definitely one every leader should strive towards. The least important word when it comes to leadership is the word 'I', the most important word is the word 'we' and one of the most powerful and often least spoken sentences a leader can say is, *it was my fault, I am sorry*. If you really want to powerfully motivate your people and truly produce works of excellence, then as a leader you must be prepared to give others credit, recognition, let your team receive a standing ovation instead of you basking in the limelight on stage. Leaders that truly build long lasting, trusting relationships celebrate the achievements and hard work of their team members, they know their success was not theirs, it was the team's success. On the other hand, when something goes wrong, the truly great leaders do not look to blame the team, they point the finger directly at themselves first and ask the question, where did I go wrong? This is powerful, this is true leadership.

The Importance of Alignment

The power of trust is about trusting ourselves, trusting others and gaining other people's trust in our leadership. Deep levels of trust can truly flourish in an environment of happiness. Happiness is the soil in which the flower of trust can grow. If you are not happy within yourself, then you do not like yourself and you will suffer from a sense of low self-worth, you will end up doubting and mistrusting yourself. We all give out a certain energy and vibration, a leader that is full of doubt about themselves will not be able to gain the full trust of their team, people will pick up on that leader's lack of self-confidence. Fully confident, happy, energetic and passionate leaders give out an energy that sends a powerful message to other people which gains their trust. Being happy as a leader is important and happiness can be defined in many different ways. I would like to give you a very useful definition of happiness that you can apply to yourself and the people you lead. Patrick Bet-David, an American entrepreneur, author and host of you tube channel 'Valuetainment', defines happiness as '*alignment*'.

Being happy is when what you want your desires, ambitions, goals and dreams, whichever word you want to use, to be aligned with the amount of effort, work and endeavour that you are putting in to achieve those wants. If your desires and your actions match up, you will be happy. Let's say you really want to lose weight and you are unhappy with the way your body looks but you are unwilling to give up eating unhealthy food, then there a misalignment between what you really want and what you are doing. This misalignment will make you unhappy, but as soon as you start to go to the gym and control your diet, you will begin to move yourself towards being aligned with what you really want, this principle applies to almost any aspect of our lives. Sometimes we do not know what we really want but we are putting in lots of effort and taking lots of action, but all that expended energy can still leave us feeling miserable if it is not in the direction of what we really want. Alignment is very much linked to being congruent. The starting point of happiness in any aspect of your life, will be working out what it is you actually want.

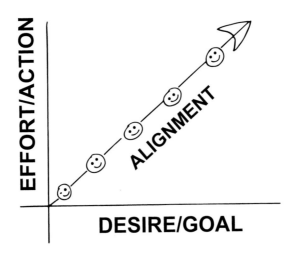

I regularly coach a wide variety of leaders from diverse fields, many of whom have exceled in their professions or chosen areas of expertise, however, they still feel unfulfilled and it is common to discover that they do not really know what they want. I work with them to find these deeper answers through the powerful *'BE GREAT'* coaching tool I have developed. Unhappy leaders can create many problems for those around them, they can create an environment of insecurity and mistrust because that is what they feel deep within themselves, their efforts are not aligned to their desires because they do not want to make the

145

effort to get what they want or, they are making lots of effort but do not really know what they want. A key question to ask yourself as a leader is, am I aligned? Or to put it another way, what do I want? Do my actions reflect what I really want?

Are the people you lead aligned? Are they happy? Effective leaders take the time to really understand what their people want. Many times, a leader may spot great potential in someone and pushes them in a certain direction out of a genuine sense of wanting to help that person reach their potential. However, if it's not the direction they really want to go, pushing them will not help. 'You can take a horse to water but you can't make it drink', the horse has to be thirsty! As a leader, forcing issues on other people never works, rather it can create feelings of resentment and mistrust. The more aligned your people are at work, the happier and more productive they will be. If you discover that a person is not truly happy at work, despite your best efforts, it is better for them and ultimately better for the business, if they were to accept the situation and leave the company. Misaligned people are never good for business.

The Ultimate Aim of Leadership

'In the joy of others, lies our own,
In the good of others, lies our own,
In the progress of others, lies our own'
His Holiness Pramukh Swami Maharaj

I have been immensely blessed in my life to have come into contact with my spiritual guide and Guru, His Holiness Pramukh Swami Maharaj. He was someone that exemplified true leadership at its highest and most profound level. He was not a person of eloquent words but his life and actions spoke volumes. His life transformed people. Simplicity, wisdom and striking humility radiated from his being. Being in his presence one would feel an immense sense of peace, bliss and divinity. Once a Christian man who had experienced some personal tragedies in his life came to Pramukh Swami Maharaj for guidance and solace. This man had lost his faith. Pramukh Swami Maharaj, despite being a Hindu guru, did not suggest this man become a Hindu. Instead, he listened carefully to the man's sorrows and gently advised him to regain his faith by attending his church regularly, reading his bible and donating to his church whenever he could.

147

We live in a world where so many leaders are desperate to convert people to their way of seeing the world, however truly great leaders help people to find and follow the path that is right for them.

Ultimately, your effectiveness as a leader comes down to how well you can help to grow and develop your people into leaders. Great leaders grow leaders. They create the right environment in which people can realise their own potential, an environment in which each individual's natural gifts and talents can truly flourish. Leaders need to trust their people first. They need to allow them the room to experiment, innovate and be creative without being stifled or feeling fearful. It has been noted that entrepreneurs and employees sometimes have very different mindsets. An entrepreneur works with passion and ownership, they are constantly learning and innovating. An employee works by carrying out the tasks that is assigned to them by the boss and when it comes to the end of their shift they are ready to leave and not give work a second thought. Imagine how motivated, innovative and productive the people you lead could be, if you could foster an entrepreneurial mindset within them. The key to this is trusting people, giving them ownership and creating an environment where it is OK to experiment and make mistakes. Mistakes are not mistakes, they are learning lessons and the potential laboratory of innovation.

Find out your WHY for being a leader and discover the WHY of the people that you lead. People are motivated by purpose and meaning. Understand that leadership is primarily about the emotions that the leader creates within the people who they lead. Learn to harness the immense power of positive emotions to drive motivation and productivity. Master your own thoughts, emotions, words and actions so that you can be a powerful and effective leader and create those personal habits that make you a congruent individual. Deal with crisis, change and pressure effectively by being prepared and guiding your team towards the vision. Harness the immense power of trust by making sure you delegate effectively, work on keeping your team aligned and develop leaders that take ownership. This is a summary of the five powerful secrets we have journeyed through together.

I hope that the adventure has made you reflect on your leadership style and provided you with the tools to take your business, your organization, your family and your personal life to the next level.

Remember, just as it is important to not be too harsh on the people that we lead, it is also important not to be too harsh on yourself, as a leader you will make mistakes. In the process of leading others, you will discover many things about yourself and about others. Sometimes the leadership adventure will be painful as you will have to face your own weaknesses and sometimes the journey will bring you great joy and satisfaction when you achieve results and see other people develop. Keep the spirit of being a learner not a leader in your heart, at times be a leader and at times be a follower. The leadership adventure is a journey of discovery and the value of any journey is how it changes you and who you become whilst on the adventure.

Summary Key Points & Self Reflection

1. List some practical steps you can take to improve your delegation skills.

   _____

   _____

   _____

   _____

2. Describe your typical day. How do you feel at the end of the day? Do you feel like you have added value as a leader?

   _____

   _____

   _____

   _____

3. How much time do you spend on strategic, 'bigger picture' tasks? What are you going change to allow yourself to be more strategic?

   _____

   _____

   _____

   _____

4. How do you feel delegating important tasks to your team?

_____

_____

_____

_____

5. How are you going to create a better circle of trust within your team?

_____

_____

_____

_____

6. As a leader, what are three MOST important things for you personally as a result of reading this book?

_____

_____

_____

_____

Notes

DO YOU WANT TO IMPROVE YOUR LEADERSHIP, MOTIVATION OR MINDSET?

Motivational Speaking Engagements

Leadership Training Workshops

Leadership Coaching

Key Note Talks

Life Coaching

To find out how Hiten can help you reach your next level

Email – hbhatt@begreattraining.com

Contact – 07817 899 762

Hiten Bhatt   begreatnow   be_great_training